THE TASTE OF OUR TIME

Collection planned and directed by

ALBERT SKIRA

INTRODUCTION AND CONCLUSION
LÉON DEGAND
★
HISTORICAL AND CRITICAL STUDY
DENIS ROUART
★
Translated by James Emmons

CLAUDE MONET

SKIRA

Title page:
The Floating Studio (fragment), c. 1874. Rijksmuseum
Kröller-Müller, Otterlo.

★

After an eclipse of several decades, Monet is returning to favor and we are witnessing today a widespread revival of interest in his work. It was to Léon Degand, one of the most zealous champions of contemporary art, that we first turned for an evaluation of Monet's achievement and an assessment of his influence, particularly on the younger generation of painters. Before he had had time to write more than a few pages, he was cut off in the prime of life by a sudden illness. These, his last writings, throw new light on the vexed question of Monet's position in the history of modern painting. We publish them here, in the form of an Introduction and a Conclusion, and dedicate them to his memory. We are grateful to Denis Rouart, who grew up in impressionist circles and was an intimate of Monet's in the last years at Giverny, for having taken over the work at this point and written the historical and critical study which forms the central portion of the book.

CHRONOLOGICAL SURVEY

1840 **Birth of Claude-Oscar Monet on November 14 in Paris, Rue Laffitte. He was the elder son of a grocer.**

1839 Birth of Cézanne and Sisley.
1840 Birth of Rodin and Odilon Redon.
1841 Birth of Renoir, Bazille, Guillaumin and Berthe Morisot.

1845 **The Monet family moves to Le Havre, on the Channel coast. There young Monet spends a happy childhood, in daily contact with the sea, under the vast, ever-changing skies of Normandy. In his teens he acquires a precocious reputation as a caricaturist.**

1855 Paris World's Fair. Pissarro, aged 25, arrives in Paris from the Antilles, where he was born.

1858 **Monet's decisive meeting with Eugène Boudin, who orients him toward landscape and open-air painting. "All of a sudden it was like a veil torn from my eyes and I understood at last, I realized what painting could be; thanks to the example of this painter, enamored of his art and practising it in his own way, my own destiny as a painter opened up before me."**

1859 **Goes to Paris in May. Meets Troyon, who gives him friendly advice. Studies at the Académie Suisse, where he meets Pissarro, and spends his evenings at the Brasserie des Martyrs.**

1859 June. Courbet and Baudelaire at Honfleur with Boudin.

1860 **April. Monet paints landscapes at Champigny-sur-Marne. Autumn. Leaves for military service in Algeria.**

1860 Large-scale Exhibition of Modern Painting in Paris (Delacroix, Corot, Courbet, Millet).
1861 Cézanne comes to Paris, meets Pissarro at the Académie Suisse.

1862 **Discharged from the army early in the year, Monet returns to Le Havre and lives at home. During the summer he works at Sainte-Adresse with Boudin and makes the acquaintance of Jongkind.**
November. Returns to Paris and enters Gleyre's studio where he meets Renoir, Sisley and Bazille.

1863 April. During the Easter holidays Monet and Bazille go down to Chailly-en-Bière in Fontainebleau Forest and paint in the open air.
December. Gleyre shuts down his studio.
1863 Salon des Refusés, which brings Manet into the limelight. Death of Delacroix.

1864 Spring. Paints at Chailly with Bazille, Renoir and Sisley. Meets Courbet in Paris. Spends the summer and autumn at Honfleur, where Bazille joins him for a few weeks.

1865 Shares Bazille's Paris studio, 5, Rue de Furstenberg. Exhibits two seascapes at the Salon. Spends the summer with Bazille at Chailly, where he paints his "Déjeuner sur l'herbe." Renoir and Sisley work nearby at Marlotte. Autumn at Trouville with Daubigny, Courbet and Whistler.
1865 Manet exhibits "Olympia."

1866 Views of Paris. Zola praises his portrait of Camille, "Woman in a Green Dress," exhibited at the Salon. Lives and works at Ville-d'Avray ("Women in the Garden"), then at Le Havre ("Terrace near Le Havre"), then at Honfleur.
1866 The Goncourt brothers publish "Manette Salomon."

1867 Virtually penniless, Monet lives with his aunt, Madame Lecadre, at Sainte-Adresse, while in Paris Camille gives birth to a son, Jean Monet. Returns to Paris in the autumn and stays with Bazille, 1, Rue Visconti.
1867 Paris World's Fair. Death of Baudelaire.

1868 Lives and works at Bonnières-sur-Seine, Fécamp, Etretat.
1868-1870 Gatherings of painters and writers at the Café Guerbois.

1869 Settles in June at Saint-Michel, near Bougival. Renoir is in the neighborhood and they often work together. Each paints three versions of "La Grenouillère."

1870 Monet and Camille Doncieux are married on June 26 and spend the summer at Trouville. Outbreak of the Franco-Prussian War on July 18. In September Monet takes refuge in London where, through Daubigny, he meets the dealer Paul Durand-Ruel.
1870 Bazille killed in action at Beaune-la-Rolande (November 28).

1871 Pissarro joins him in London and together they visit the museums. Makes a trip to Holland (Zaandam). Discovers Japanese prints and buys some. Returns to France by way of Antwerp. In December he settles at Argenteuil.

1872 Spring at Le Havre ("Impression, Sunrise"). Second trip to Holland in the summer.

1873 At Argenteuil he becomes friendly with the amateur painter Gustave Caillebotte. Fits up a studio on his boat, from which he paints the banks of the Seine.

1874 Monet, Renoir and Manet work together at Argenteuil. Manet gives him financial assistance.

1874 April 15-May 15. First Group Exhibition at Nadar's, 35, Boulevard des Capucines.

1875 Dire financial straits and illness of Camille.

1875 March 24. Auction sale of works by Monet, Sisley, Renoir and Berthe Morisot at the Hôtel Drouot.

1876 Meets the collector Victor Chocquet. Summer stay with the financier and collector Ernest Hoschedé and his wife at the Château de Montgeron (Seine-et-Oise), where he paints a decoration entitled "Turkeys."
Winter. In Paris, begins his "Gare Saint-Lazare" series.

1876 April. Second Group Exhibition at Durand-Ruel's, 11, Rue Le Peletier.

1877 Second stay with the Hoschedés at Montgeron. Winter in Paris.

1877 April. Third Group Exhibition at 6, Rue Le Peletier.
May 28. Second auction sale of impressionist paintings, in which Monet takes no part.
Gatherings at the Café de la Nouvelle-Athènes. Death of Courbet.

1878 Leaves Argenteuil and rents a house at Vétheuil, further down the Seine, where he settles in the spring, after the birth of his second son Michel (March). Hoschedé's business ventures collapse and he is ruined; his family is taken in by Monet.

1878 Paris World's Fair. Death of Daubigny.
Théodore Duret publishes "Les peintres impressionnistes."

1879 September. Death of Camille.
Winter. Paints views of the ice on the Seine.
1879 April 10-May 11. Fourth Group Exhibition at 28, Avenue de l'Opéra.

1880 June. One-man show (18 pictures) in the offices of the review "La Vie Moderne," 7, Boulevard des Italiens.
1880 April. Fifth Group Exhibition at 10, Rue des Pyramides. Disagreements between Monet and Degas. Sponsored by Pissarro, Gauguin shows with the group.

1881 Works at Vétheuil and Fécamp. In December, settles at Poissy, living with Madame Hoschedé and her children.
1881 April. Sixth Group Exhibition at 35, Boulevard des Capucines (Monet abstains).

1882 Works on the Channel coast at Varengeville, Dieppe and Pourville.
1882 March. Seventh Group Exhibition at 251, Rue Saint-Honoré.

1883 January and February in Le Havre and Etretat. One-man show in March at Durand-Ruel's (56 items). Settles at Giverny in May, renting a house which he later buys (1890). Trip to the Riviera in December with Renoir; they pay a visit to Cézanne at L'Estaque.
1883 April 30. Death of Manet.

1884 From January 17 to April 14, revisits the Riviera, alone this time, working first at Bordighera, then at Menton. August at Etretat on the Channel coast with his family.
1884 Founding of the "Société des Indépendants" and its yearly Salon.

1885 Exhibits at the Galerie Georges Petit. Quarrels with Durand-Ruel. Works at Etretat from October to December.

1886 Brief trip to Holland in April. September at Belle-Ile, off the coast of Brittany, where he meets Gustave Geffroy. November with Octave Mirbeau on the island of Noirmoutier, off the coast of the Vendée department.
1886 May 15-June 15. Eighth and last Group Exhibition at 1, Rue Laffitte, with the participation of Seurat and Signac at the insistence of Pissarro. Van Gogh arrives in Paris.

1888 January-April. Works at Antibes on the Riviera. Trip to London in July. September at Etretat painting the cliffs and fishing-boats on the beach. His Mediterranean paintings are warmly praised by Mallarmé.

1888 Gauguin and Van Gogh at Arles.

1889 Spring at Fresselines in the Creuse department.
June. Monet-Rodin Exhibition at the Galerie Georges Petit.

1889 Bergson publishes "Les données immédiates de la conscience."

1890 First series of "Poplars" and "Haystacks."
Buys the house he has been renting at Giverny and embarks on the creation of his famous water-garden.

1890 Death of Van Gogh at Auvers-sur-Oise.

1891 More "Poplars" and "Haystacks." Exhibition in May at Durand-Ruel's. Trip to London in December.

1891 Death of Seurat. Gauguin leaves for Tahiti.

1892 Works at Rouen in February and March, painting the cathedral. Exhibition at Durand-Ruel's in early March. Monet and Madame Hoschedé are married in the summer.

1893 Works on the "Cathedrals," first at Rouen in February and March, then at Giverny, from memory, for the rest of the year.

1893 Exhibition of Japanese art at Durand-Ruel's.

1894 Cézanne pays a visit to Giverny in November and Monet introduces him to Rodin, Clemenceau and Geffroy.

1894 Death of Caillebotte, who leaves a large collection of impressionist paintings to the State; Renoir is named executor of . his will.

1895 January. Trip to Norway, staying at Sandviken, near Oslo.
May. Exhibits 50 works at Durand-Ruel's.
June. Water-cure at Salies-de-Béarn in the Pyrenees.

1895 Death of Berthe Morisot. Cézanne Exhibition at Vollard's.

1896 February-March. Works at Varengeville and Pourville on the Channel coast, painting the cliffs.

1896 Pissarro paints at Rouen. Bonnard Exhibition at Durand-Ruel's.

1897 Again at Pourville from January to March.

1897 Pissarro paints in London.

1898 June. Large exhibition at the Galerie Georges Petit.

1898 Death of Mallarmé.

1899 Summer. Paints water lilies in the pond in his garden. Autumn. Visit to London, begins a series of views of the Thames.

1899 Death of Sisley. Nabi Exhibition at Durand-Ruel's.

1900 February. Another trip to London, where he is visited by Clemenceau and Geffroy. Returns to Giverny in April, works at Vétheuil during the summer. November 22-December 15. Exhibition at Durand-Ruel's.

1900 Paris World's Fair with a large exhibition of French art.

1901 February-April. In London working on his Thames series.

1901 Death of Lautrec. Van Gogh Retrospective Exhibition.

1902 Visit to Brittany in February and March.

1902 Death of Zola. Lautrec Retrospective Exhibition.

1903 Finishes his Thames series at Giverny from memory. Buys an automobile.

1903 Death of Gauguin and Pissarro. Founding of the Salon d'Automne.

1904 May 9-June 4. Exhibits 37 views of the Thames at Durand-Ruel's. Summer. Paints his water-garden at Giverny and ''Water Lilies.'' October. Drives to Madrid with his wife to see Velazquez' paintings in the Prado.

1904 Renoir and Cézanne rooms at the Salon d'Automne.

1906 Works all year on his ''Water Lilies.''

1906 Death of Cézanne. Gauguin Retrospective.

1908 Illness and eye trouble. From September to December, first visit to Venice, accompanied by his wife. There, recovering his health and good spirits, he paints with renewed enthusiasm.

1909 May 6-June 5. Exhibition of 48 ''Water Lilies'' at Durand-Ruel's. A great success. Second trip to Venice in the autumn.

1910 Begins a new series of ''Water Lilies.''

1911 Death of Madame Monet (May 19). From now on Monet seldom leaves the solitude of Giverny where, despite failing eyesight, he works on unremittingly, painting his garden and water lilies.

1912 May 28-June 8. Exhibits 29 views of Venice at Bernheim-Jeune's.

1914 Death of Jean Monet (February 10), whose widow, Blanche Hoschedé, henceforth keeps house for Monet.

1916 Begins his large decorative panels of "Water Lilies," commissioned by Clemenceau for the State.

1917 October. Last visit to the Channel coast: Honfleur, Le Havre, Etretat, Yport, Pourville and Dieppe.

1917 Death of Degas.
1919 Death of Renoir.

1921 January 21-February 2. Retrospective Monet Exhibition at Durand-Ruel's.
September. Brief visit to Brittany.

1922 Suffering from a double cataract.

1922 Death of Durand-Ruel.

1923 An operation partially restores his sight and he is able to put the last touches on the decorative panels of "Water Lilies." These were installed after his death in the oval rooms especially designed for them in the Musée de l'Orangerie in Paris.

1926 Death of Monet at Giverny, December 5, aged 86.

INTRODUCTION

W hen about *1855-1857* Claude Monet, still in his teens, first acquired a few rudimentary ideas about the art of painting, what was the position of that art in France? What were the obstacles a young, imaginative painter might be expected to come up against?

The Old Masters had one by one receded into a limbo remote from contemporary life, and with them had receded certain strictly compositional problems. This was all to the good: the role of academicism, ineluctably, in every age, is that of devouring its own offspring and thereby disqualifying, for an indeterminate period, a number of principles which, none the less, had proved their validity.

A heated controversy was about to lose its virulence and pass into history. The antagonists were, on the one hand, a (figuratively speaking) blind devotee of Raphael and pictorial conventions deriving almost entirely from the externals of his art; on the other, a thorough-paced "romantic," an ardent admirer of Rubens and the *16th*-century Venetians. For the one, perfection of line was all that mattered; he regarded color as mere "filling," little more than an accessory of flawless draftsmanship. For the other, the splendors of color were the be-all and end-all of painting; line was merely hinted at. In practice, needless to say, the first was a highly skillful colorist and the second a draftsman of great verve and acumen. The Cubists were later to pay homage to the first, whose work, in their eyes, anthologized the wonders that could be done with planes and lines. But, pending the advent of Cubism, it *was the second, very early in his career, who was destined to make the discovery on which so much of the coming renewal of painting depended.*

At the 1824 Salon, in Paris, among a number of landscapes by contemporary English painters, Delacroix (for he, of course, is the second artist referred to, and Ingres is the first) noticed three landscapes by Constable and was struck by the intensity of certain tones which, at a distance, merged together uniformly. Examining the canvases, he saw that these tones, applied in small, separate brushstrokes, owed their intensity to their division into shades of the same tone. This new technique invented by an English artist was the prelude of an art revolution, on the other side of the Channel, in which Monet was to play a heroic part.

Much has been made of both Ingres and Delacroix as precursors of modern art. The fact remains that both were staunchly orthodox exponents of an art conceived and executed in the image of the Old Masters, in accordance with the canons of the "classical" schools of Renaissance painting. But they were seized on and idealized by certain moderns who, with a modesty that cloaked no little pride, declared themselves the true continuators of the masters of the past.

In the case of Ingres and Delacroix that debt to the past was apportioned between a small number of Old Masters. Not so with the average run of painters, who carried Eclecticism to extravagant lengths. Ransacking the whole field of art, they picked on formulas which seemed to them the acme of perfection in some shape or form; then, mixing them together, they produced a composite art, a hotchpotch, whose overall effect was insipid to a degree. Such, in brief, was what the contemporary methods of teaching art promoted; such was the normal approach to an understanding and appreciation of painting a hundred years ago, and this was the kind of initiation which a novice, seized by the ambition to paint, was most liable to undergo. Monet was no exception; his first still lifes were the fruit of just such an initiation.

But there is one category of painters which suffered less than others from this occupational disease: the votaries of pure landscape—Corot,

16

the Barbizon painters, and others like Paul Huet. It cannot be said that these men owed nothing to their predecessors; they had little to say that was really new. Straight landscape painting, after all, was not their invention. Rubens had tried his hand at it long before the romantics of Fontainebleau Forest or anywhere else. Nor were the 17th-century Dutch masters wholly unfamiliar with it. Corot, in fact, made so thorough a study of Ruisdael that he took over from him, quite unwittingly, the practice of enhancing a symphony of greens with a discreet dab of vivid red. Bonington had enjoyed much success in Paris, and at the 1824 Salon the English landscapists by no means passed unnoticed. It is worth noting, however, that Turner was unrepresented at that famous Salon.

But the new school of French landscape painting, in the mid-19th century, nevertheless had to its credit one rare and precious asset: a pure, unsophisticated love of nature (except when Corot began exploiting the "poetic" mists hovering over the meres of Ville-d'Avray). They no longer "staged" their landscapes, and in this they took after the Dutch masters. They kept clear of the scenic effects of vaporous parks with shepherds and shepherdesses playing their dainty parts in a pastoral idyll or scène galante. *Their trees were neither conventional accessories nor stock motifs, their fields were racy of the soil. Enthusiastically, with no sense of inferiority, they practised a genre which the School, defender of traditional categories, regarded as a minor branch of art. In the end, thanks to them, those watertight categories, and all the prejudices that went with them, were abolished. They pioneered the liberation of painting from at least one shackle: from the theater, from scenery and stage effects. And it was not only painting and painters that benefited by this liberation, for what was actually taking place was the triumph of "nature," the triumph in all walks of life of a new response to the visible world, and a rejection of outworn theatrical conventions. In spite of the fact that for decades to come painters clung desperately to old-fashioned conceptions of "nature," it was by this devious means that painting worked its way toward the full realization of its own specifically pictorial possibilities.*

The marvel of it is that the authors of this little revolution were unaware of the implications of their exploit—but a marvel in perfect keeping with the ease and naturalness with which it was brought off.

With respect to the Old Masters and even to Ingres and Delacroix, the new school of French landscape painting presented another peculiarity. Owing perhaps to the very fact that they no longer had to adapt the landscape to religious or mythological figures playing the leading role in the picture, but concentrated solely on a (more or less) spontaneous depiction of nature, they no longer troubled themselves about composing pictures based on geometric principles. They continued to compose, of course, but they chose their patterns with an eye to pictorial rhythm, and were thereby led to seek out new rhythms.

Another thing: though they painted a good deal in the open air, they always produced the finished picture in the studio. In this respect they conformed to a centuries-old tradition. Constable himself, though he rejuvenated the art of landscape by his many open-air sketches, fully worked out in every detail, never executed pictures intended for exhibition anywhere but in the studio. The working habits of painters at that time, and indeed their whole psychological make-up, were such that it was impossible for them to regard a canvas painted out of doors, at the mercy of wind and weather, as a "real" picture.

Lastly, to return to Monet, a great lesson in modernism was in store for him when he first went to Paris in 1859: the lesson of Courbet, who had eliminated angels from painting—since, as he said, he had never seen any—and replaced them by such human beings as he had seen. Courbet was the champion of realism in its most positive form. It all seemed very strange and rather shocking at the time, but he did much to open the eyes of progressive-minded painters to subjects which, though not "noble," were nevertheless worthy of interest. For all his gifts, however, Courbet never freed himself (except in a few seascapes) from the old eclecticism, from an art of set formulas culled from the time-honored masterpieces in the museums—and from the repertory of the Schools. The truth is that Courbet innovated only in his choice of subjects. In the matter of purely pictorial expression, his technique and formal language constituted a throw-back to old-fashioned methods. There was no end to the relics and reminiscences which he lumped together and shaped (very skillfully, be it said) to his own ends. But the younger painters, eager for novelty, were astonished and fascinated by the vigorous, overt traces of his brush (so different from the slick technique of the academics) in the dense pigment of his canvases. Such brushwork was nothing new; it had been used by the Dutch masters two centuries before Courbet was born. No matter; to young painters a hundred years ago it came as a complete surprise.

This, then, was what Paris held in store for young Monet, fresh from a country town in Normandy: a few openings, and a great many obstacles. To some extent, however, he came forearmed, for the enlightenment that most newcomers hoped to find in Paris Monet had already found, thanks to the guidance of an unassuming provincial painter: Eugène Boudin.

Boudin painted simply and unpretentiously, but he was in love with his subjects: the sea and ships, the beaches, the Channel ports, most of all the sky. He never minimized the importance of the sky, never dismissed it as a mere background. Boudin knew very well (though he was not the man to theorize about it) that the painter's depth of feeling, his joie de peindre, *does not depend on the "nobility" of his subject, or on his success with dealers and collectors. He was enraptured by those aspects of nature which were his chosen subjects. He never failed to respect their outward appearances, but his very devotion to nature led him to transpose and refashion her image, diffidently but with great finesse. Out of a desire perhaps to surrender himself to her more fully, he took to painting in the open. To those accustomed to painting nature only from memory, in the seclusion of the studio, with the help of studies jotted down outdoors, this must have seemed a very rash step. But Boudin took it, confident that for him it was the only approach to nature, indeed the only valid approach to painting. What is important to note is that Boudin not only painted outdoors (there was nothing new in that), but painted each canvas from start to finish outdoors, which was revolutionary. And which contributed to the brightening of his palette—another innovation at the time.*

Such was the example which Boudin set and which young Monet gladly followed. From a caricaturist he became a landscapist, his eyes were opened to bright colors and he was initiated into open-air painting. He thus made a decisive forward step while still in his teens, without having to wrestle with the hidebound disciplines of a school. The museums and studios of Paris, the set rules and tricks of the trade—he was initiated into all that afterwards. *There is no overlooking this exceptional psychological advantage.*

LÉON DEGAND.

YOUTH AND EARLY TRAINING

THE year 1840 was the middle year of three which were particularly important for the future of French painting. In that brief period seven of the major artists destined to launch the impressionist movement were born: Cézanne and Sisley in 1839, Monet in 1840, Berthe Morisot, Guillaumin, Renoir and Bazille in 1841.

On November 14, 1840, two days after the birth of Rodin, Claude-Oscar Monet was born in Paris, Rue Laffitte. The family moved in 1845 to Le Havre, in Normandy, where Monet's father, entering into partnership with his brother-in-law, Monsieur Lecadre, hoped to make a fresh start in the grocery business. The boy was five years old at the time. The sea thus became the constant background of his whole childhood, and he spent more time roaming the beaches than in the schoolroom. "I was born undisciplined," wrote Monet. "Never, even as a child, could I be made to obey a set rule. What little I know I learned at home. School was always like a prison to me, I could never bring myself to stay there, even four hours a day, when the sun was shining and the sea was so tempting, and it was such fun scrambling over cliffs and paddling in the shallows. Such, to the great despair of my parents, was the unruly but healthy life I lived until I was fourteen or fifteen. In the meantime I somehow picked up the rudiments of reading, writing and arithmetic, with a smattering of spelling. And there my schooling ended. It never worried me very much because I always had plenty of amusements on the side. I doodled in the margins of my books, I decorated our blue copy paper with ultra-fantastic drawings, and I drew the faces and profiles of my schoolmasters as outrageously as I could, distorting them out of all recognition."

It is important to remember young Monet's aversion for the "prison" of the schoolroom and his love of the out-of-doors where he could roam at will, for they reflected a passionate longing to be free. Such was his nature then, and such it remained all his life. He did not, however, so easily discover his true vocation, but began with caricature, an art form essentially concerned with the human face and utterly indifferent to the beauties of nature.

"At fifteen I was known all over Le Havre as a caricaturist. My reputation was so well established that from all sides people came to me and pestered me for caricatures. I had so many requests, and the pocket money my mother could spare me was so meager, that I was led to take a bold step, one which needless to say shocked my parents: I started selling my portraits. Sizing up my customer, I charged ten or twenty francs a caricature, and it worked like a charm. Within a month my clientele had doubled. Had I gone on like that I'd be a millionaire today. Soon I was looked up to in the town, I was 'somebody'. In the shop-window of the one and only frame-maker who could eke out a livelihood in Le Havre, my caricatures were impudently displayed, five or six abreast, in beaded frames or behind glass like very fine works of art, and when I saw troops of bystanders gazing at them in admiration, pointing at them and crying 'Why, that's so-and-so!', I was just bursting with pride."

It was Boudin who oriented Monet's budding talents and brought them into line with his love of nature and freedom. This occurred in the following way. In his shop-window, alongside the caricatures, the frame-maker also displayed some seascapes which young Monet dismissed as "awful daubs." The author of them, Eugène Boudin, an ex-sailor with a passion for painting, was the man who opened the store in the first place; among his customers were Troyon and Millet.

Once Boudin had come in contact with them, it was not long before he passed on the business to someone else and devoted himself to painting. In 1851 he had received a municipal grant enabling him to study art in Paris for three years. He came back to Le Havre convinced that the romantics had had their day and that it was high time for a return to nature.

When Boudin saw Monet's caricatures, he realized that the youngster had genuine talent. He made inquiries about him in the shop and the frame-maker tried to arrange a meeting between them. But Monet showed no interest and even went out of his way to avoid Boudin, till one day, by chance, they ran into each other at the frame-maker's. The shopkeeper seized the opportunity and introduced them. "Boudin came over at once and started talking to me in his soft voice, saying nice things about my work: 'I like your sketches, they're very amusing, very neatly done. You're gifted, anybody can see that. But you're not going to stop there, I hope. This is all right for a start, but you'll soon have had your fill of caricature. You want to buckle down and study hard, learn to see and paint, go out and sketch, do some landscapes. What beauty there is in the sea and sky, in animals, people and trees, just as nature made them, just as they are, with a character of their own, with a life of their own in the light and air of nature.' But Boudin's advice was lost on me. As for the man himself, I couldn't help liking him. He meant what he said, he was sincere all right, I felt that. But I couldn't stomach his painting, and whenever he offered to take me out sketching with him in the open country, I always had some pretext or other for a polite refusal. Summer came, my time was more or less my own, I could hardly put him off any longer. So to get it over with I gave in and Boudin, with unfailing kindness, took me in hand. In the end my eyes were opened and I gained a real understanding of nature, and a real love of her as well."

Elsewhere, in another account of his youthful initiation, Monet described it as "a bolt from the blue." "All of a sudden it was like a veil torn from my eyes and I understood at last, I realized what painting could be." But whether progressive or sudden it was a twofold revelation, both of painting and nature, of each in terms of the other. This is a point of cardinal importance, for apart from a few brief excursions into other fields Monet's entire body of work was oriented toward nature. "If I have become a painter, I owe it to Boudin."

Boudin was thirty-four, Monet seventeen. Throughout the summer of 1858 they painted together, directly from nature. In his efforts to capture the freshness and spontaneity of his initial sensation, Boudin turned out sketch after sketch, and it was these which Baudelaire described as "studies so rapidly, so faithfully registering the most transient and elusive states of form and color, of waves and clouds." Instead of painting conventional clouds, Boudin endeavored to record their most fleeting aspects. To do so, he had to work out a technique rapid and flexible enough to capture every hue and nuance of that element in perpetual metamorphosis—the sky.

Boudin not only set Monet the example but gave him sensible advice, always in clear and simple terms. "The first impression is the right one, be just as stubborn as you can in sticking to it... Whatever is painted directly, on the spot, always has a vigor, a power, a vivacity of touch that can't be recovered in the studio... Three brushstrokes from nature are worth more than two days' work at the easel."

But Monet realized that the teaching and example of a single master, however admirable, was not enough; that he needed to broaden his horizon, to confront and compare his work with that of others. "It's no good persevering in isolation, unless of course one is supremely gifted, and even then you cannot expect to invent an art all by yourself, in a country town, cut off from criticism and points of comparison, with nothing but your own instinct to guide you." Thus stimulated by Boudin, Monet was eager to go to Paris, visit the exhibitions and frequent the studios. His father accordingly applied to the Municipal Council of Le Havre for a grant, such as Boudin had received eight years earlier.

This was in 1859. After two months the application was rejected. The worthy aldermen of Le Havre felt that his caricatures failed to show any aptitude for the more serious, more laborious studies which alone could qualify for municipal largess. Perhaps too they had misgivings about the sponsorship of Boudin who, in their eyes, had betrayed the trust which the municipality had placed in him.

Luckily, thanks to the sale of his caricatures, Monet had saved up enough to go to Paris anyhow, and from there he wrote long letters to Boudin giving his impressions of the paintings he saw. He was severe and clairvoyant in his judgments of many great academic names of that day, all of whom are now forgotten. Of Delacroix, on the other hand, he had this to say: "They are only jottings, rough sketches, but as always what vitality, what movement in them!" Of Daubigny: "Now there's a fellow who does good work, who understands nature." And further: "The Corots are simply marvels." All his comments show that Monet was already keenly alive to the luminosity of skies, already critical of very dark shadows.

He was advised by Troyon to enter the studio of Couture, whose painting, however, Monet found so distasteful to him that he opted for one of the free schools, the Académie Suisse, where he met Pissarro. He seems to have neglected his work a little for the Brasserie des Martyrs, where he fell in with a group of painters and writers. There, pitted against classicists and romantics, the realists upheld the artist's right to paint contemporary life just as he saw it, unhampered by the conventional obsession with mythological, antique and medieval subjects. The writers Duranty, Castagnary and Champfleury presided over the discussions, and Baudelaire and Théodore de Banville also took part in these boisterous gatherings where, in a haze of smoke, talk went on far into the night.

He later admitted that he had wasted a lot of time in the Brasserie des Martyrs and was none the better for it. His parents frowned on the Bohemian life he was leading, and when the time came for him to do his military service they refused to purchase a substitute for him. In 1860 he was conscripted and his first stay in Paris came to a close.

At that time the term of military service was fixed at seven years, but not all men were caught in the net. Each year lots were drawn to determine the contingent to be incorporated in the standing army; each conscript, however, had the option of purchasing a substitute. Monet drew an unlucky number and his father summoned him to take his choice: either to enrol at the Ecole des Beaux-Arts and follow a regular course of official instruction, or else to go into the army. Dead set against the official School, Monet declined the offer and his parents left him to his fate, in hopes that a spell of army life would do him good.

Acting on a friend's advice, he enlisted in the Chasseurs d'Afrique, light cavalry troops for African service. "I spent two really delightful years in Algeria. There were new sights to be seen all the time, and in leisure moments I tried my hand at rendering them. You can't imagine how much I learned in this way, how well it trained my eye. I wasn't aware of it myself at first. The impressions of light and color that I received down there only got sorted out later, but the seeds of my future work had already begun to sprout."

Monet was a sturdy young man but his system was not equal to the African climate and by 1862 he had fallen seriously ill. Sent home on sick leave, he set to painting again with redoubled enthusiasm. Meanwhile his father had been warned by the doctors that his son's health might suffer irremediably from another stay in Africa. Realizing that the lesson had gone far enough, and realizing too perhaps that the headstrong boy would have his own way in any event, he paid for a substitute to serve out the remaining five years of his son's enlistment.

So Monet was free again, his time was his own, and he spent it painting out of doors, very often in Boudin's company. It was now that he accidentally made the acquaintance of Jongkind who, momentarily cured of his drinking habits, was again painting at Le Havre. Working alone one day, Monet was struggling to get a cow into the pose he wanted, when an Englishman came along, gave him a hand, and asked him if he knew Jongkind; upon receiving a negative reply, he offered to introduce Monet to him.

"To my great surprise the Englishman kept his word, and on the following Sunday the three of us lunched together. What a good time we had, out of doors under the trees, in the garden of a rustic inn, with good country cooking. With a full glass in front of him, sitting between two admirers whose sincerity could not be questioned, Jongkind was beside himself with joy. It was an unexpected treat and put him in the best of humor. It was not every day that he was sought out by such admirers. His painting was too novel and struck too artistic a note for it to be appreciated in 1862 at its true value. It must be said too that no one was less of a pusher than Jongkind. He was a simple, good-hearted soul, very shy, who murdered the French language. We caught him in a very expansive mood. He asked to see some of my sketches, invited me to come out and work with him, explained the why and wherefore of his manner to me and so added the crowning touch to the encouragement Boudin had already given me. From then on my true master was Jongkind and to him I owe the education of my eye."

CAMILLE WITH A PUPPY, 1866. EMIL BÜHRLE COLLECTION, ZURICH.

EXPERIMENTS AND DISCOVERIES

PARIS - CHAILLY - HONFLEUR - VILLE-D'AVRAY - BOUGIVAL - TROUVILLE

AFTER spending the summer of 1862 painting with Jongkind on the Channel coast, Monet was eager to get back to Paris. But this time, having bought him out of the army with the proviso that he should settle down, his parents insisted on his enrolling in an official studio—otherwise his allowance would be cut off and he would have to fend for himself.

It was decided that he should consult Toulmouche, a cousin by marriage, who had become a successful painter in the slick, mawkish manner of the day. Toulmouche advised him to enter Gleyre's studio; Monet did so, and there he met Bazille, Renoir and Sisley. Similarity of outlook and temperament brought them together almost from the start. They formed a group apart in Gleyre's studio, and made good their escape from it at the first opportunity.

There are various accounts of this historic episode; they differ in detail but agree in the main as to what actually happened. It was after Gleyre had corrected a study made from the living model that Monet resolved to leave the studio. According to some accounts this incident occurred the first time Gleyre made the rounds to correct his students' work, a bare two weeks after classes had begun. But it must have been later, for it seems certain that Monet and his friends attended Gleyre's classes off and on throughout the winter of 1862-1863. After all, Monet had pledged himself to follow an official course of instruction and he knew there would be trouble with his parents if he failed to do so. Gleyre, moreover, was a liberal-minded teacher and though, according to Renoir, he was of no help whatever to his pupils, it must be said to his credit that he left them alone. In all likelihood Renoir, Bazille and Sisley would have gone on working with so indulgent a master (whom they chose of their own free will), had they not been lured away by Monet, who rebelled at Gleyre's invariable method of correcting nature in accordance with the "sacred" canons of antique art.

In the spring of 1863, accompanied by Bazille, he went down to Chailly-en-Bière for a few days to paint from nature in Fontainebleau Forest. Delighted with the place and completely absorbed by the work in hand, he prolonged his stay and let Bazille return to Paris alone.

During the previous winter in Paris, visiting the galleries and exhibitions, he had been instinctively attracted to the works of Corot and Courbet. Corot's intimate contact with nature and the purity and sincerity of his vision exemplified all the precepts of Jongkind and Boudin. Courbet's congenital realism, with its frank and rugged power, was equally agreeable to him. Then he discovered Manet, whose bold originality asserted itself in his forcible, virile handling of contrasting planes of color, with a total disregard of the smooth modeling and careful transitions prescribed in the official studios. In the years to come the example of these men served as the touchstone by which he evaluated his own progress and experience. Dividing his time between Paris, in winter, and Le Havre and Fontainebleau in summer, Monet spent the 1860s getting his bearings.

In the late summer of 1863, after working with Bazille at Chailly, he returned to Normandy where he was welcomed by Boudin and Jongkind. He went to work at Honfleur and there painted a *Farmyard* which shows the influence of Troyon.

At the end of 1863 Gleyre shut down his studio, so Monet and his friends were set free. As soon as the weather turned fine, they all went down to Chailly, which is only a mile or two from Barbizon, then the Mecca of landscape painters. Having already worked from nature under the guidance of Boudin and Jongkind, Monet took the lead and initiated his friends into an experience that was new to them. Fontainebleau

LE PAVÉ DE CHAILLY-EN-BIÈRE, C. 1865.
NY CARLSBERG GLYPTOTEK, COPENHAGEN.

Forest, however, was a different thing altogether from the Channel coast with its boundless horizons and variable atmosphere. The prospect that met the eye was static, almost oppressive, hemmed in by trees and undergrowth, and Monet found himself at grips with a new set of problems. In tackling them he and his friends had no alternative but to pattern their

31

efforts, consciously or unconsciously, on those of their Barbizon predecessors. With this difference, however: they painted their pictures out of doors from beginning to end, without touching them up in the studio afterwards, as their elders did.

In July 1864 Monet took Bazille with him to Honfleur, to the Ferme Saint-Siméon, on the cliffs outside the town, rendezvous of seascape painters on the Channel coast. There they were joined by Boudin. After Bazille returned to Paris, Monet wrote him wildly enthusiastic letters. "I'm so eager to paint everything I see that it's driving me crazy. My head's bursting with it all..." He was so much wrapped up in his work that he could not bring himself to leave. It was not till the end of the year that he returned to Paris.

At his first attempt Monet was accepted at the 1865 Salon with two seascapes: *La pointe de la Hève* and *L'embouchure de la Seine à Honfleur*. Both were noticed and favorably reviewed by the critic Paul Mantz in the Gazette des Beaux-Arts.

In the spring of the same year Monet decided that he too would make a *Déjeuner sur l'herbe*, but a *Déjeuner* painted from figures seen in the natural attitudes of picnickers in the open air, not artificially grouped as in Manet's picture. His idea was to represent a group of people just as they appear in broad daylight on a tree-shaded lawn. He went down to Fontainebleau Forest in search of the setting he had in mind and soon found a suitable clearing. There he grouped some friends around a picnic, with sunlight converging on them through the trees.

According to Monet's own account, he painted separate studies from the life, in the open, and carefully transferred these fragments to the final canvas, which was too large to allow him to work it up on the spot. His success in rendering living figures out of doors marks an advance on Manet, even though the latter's influence is evident in his frank, straightforward manner of schematizing zones of light and shadow.

LE DÉJEUNER SUR L'HERBE, 1866. HERMITAGE, LENINGRAD.

This large canvas, dated 1866, is probably a replica, with some variants, of the monumental composition Monet had embarked on the previous year, and not (as generally supposed) a preliminary sketch for it. One such sketch still exists (Museum of Modern Western Art, Moscow); of the original work only the central area and a fragment of the right have survived. This *Déjeuner sur l'herbe* is the outcome of a truly heroic aspiration on young Monet's part: to outdo Manet on his own ground and to establish once and for all the validity of open-air painting as the basis of the new esthetic. Light filtering through the trees envelops figures, leafage and the still life in a quivering embrace. The very tall man leaning against a tree on the right is Bazille; he also posed for the man lying on the ground.

On the other hand, there is an undeniable heaviness and opacity about the landscape, so that in this respect the picture falls short of Manet's. This shortcoming can be put down in part to Monet's youth and inexperience, in part to the influence of Courbet and the Barbizon School. Painted at the same time and place, *Le Pavé de Chailly*, with its rather somber colors and cold, leaden light, again betrays the influence of Courbet.

Returning to Normandy for the summer as usual, Monet saw much of Boudin, who introduced him to Courbet. The latter took an immediate liking to Monet and gave him advice and guidance. "I cherish precious memories of our friendship," wrote Monet. "Courbet was always so kind and helpful to me, even tiding me over financial crises with loans of money."

But when he returned to Chailly at summer's end to put the finishing touches on his large *Déjeuner*, Monet let himself be persuaded by Courbet to make some changes. These he so much regretted afterwards that, acting on an impulse, he deposited it with his innkeeper as security for his unpaid bills. Rolled up and abandoned in a corner of the house, the canvas suffered from damp during the winter of 1865-1866. Meanwhile Monet went back to Normandy and, painting at Honfleur and in the neighborhood of the Ferme Saint-Siméon, he produced several snowscapes, solidly, even powerfully constructed works.

By the time he got back to Chailly and unrolled his *Déjeuner*, a large strip on the edge of the canvas had been ruined by mold. Monet cut this away and preserved the central portion with the figures, but had to give up his plan of submitting it to the 1866 Salon. Instead, he turned out in a few sittings a beautiful portrait known as the *Woman in a Green Dress* or *Camille*, the name of the model (she was soon to become Monet's wife). Though badly hung, this work was nevertheless singled out for praise by Emile Zola, who wrote as follows: "I do not know Monsieur Monet, I do not think I have ever before looked at one of his pictures with any attention. Yet I feel as if I were an old friend of his, and this is because his portrait tells me a whole story of energy and truthfulness. Yes indeed, here is a temperament, here is a man in this crowd of eunuchs. Just look at the neighboring canvases and see the sorry figure they cut beside this window thrown open on nature. There is more than a realist here, there is an able, delicate interpreter who knows how to register every detail without lapsing into dryness. Look at the dress, it is solid, yet it falls softly and freely, it is alive . . ."

The satirist André Gill paid humorous but admiring tribute to it in a caricature of the portrait, captioned as follows: "Monet or Manet? Monet all right, but we owe this Monet to Manet. Bravo, Monet! Thanks, Manet!" The truth is, however, that Manet's influence is far less in evidence in the *Woman in a Green Dress* than it is in another portrait of her, side-face, in half-length, painted about the same time: *Camille with a Puppy*.

The spring and summer of 1866 were a particularly productive period for Monet. He worked out of doors almost daily, in Paris, outside the city in the Ile-de-France, and on the Channel coast. It was then that he painted the three views of Paris from the roof of the Louvre: *Saint-Germain-l'Auxerrois, Le Jardin de l'Infante* and *Le Quai du Louvre*.

Undaunted by his mishap with the *Déjeuner sur l'herbe*, he again planned out a large-scale painting, *Women in the Garden*, but made up his mind to paint it entirely out of doors. With this in view he had a trench dug in the garden of the house he had rented at Ville-d'Avray; by means of hooks, pullies and cords he could thus lower the canvas sufficiently to reach the top of it with his brush. Courbet took an interest in the project and often came out to see how the painting was getting on. One day he was surprised to find his young friend idle and told him so; Monet replied that he was waiting for the sun.

WOMEN IN THE GARDEN, 1866-1867.
LOUVRE, PARIS.

TERRACE NEAR LE HAVRE (DETAIL), 1866.
REV. T. PITCAIRN COLLECTION, BRYN ATHYN, PA.

BEACH AT SAINTE-ADRESSE, 1867. COURTESY OF THE ART INSTITUTE OF
CHICAGO, MR AND MRS LEWIS L. COBURN MEMORIAL COLLECTION.

Courbet suggested that in the meantime he might fill in the
background. But Monet refused to touch the canvas till the
sun came out, for he felt that he could only secure the truthfulness and homogeneity he aimed at by painting all parts
of the picture under the same lighting. This incident illustrates
the difference between Courbet's realism and that of Monet.

At the end of the summer, hounded by creditors, Monet had to leave Ville-d'Avray. He was able to take *Women in the Garden* with him but preferred to destroy a large number of smaller canvases rather than let them be sold off at auction. His debts compelled him to take refuge at Le Havre. There he remained throughout the autumn and painted, among other things, a *View of the Harbor at Honfleur* and *Terrace near Le Havre*, built up in irregular planes of light and shadow, a technique which he borrowed from Manet.

THE JETTY AT LE HAVRE, 1868.
COLLECTION MR AND MRS HUNTINGTON HARTFORD, NEW YORK.

His liaison with Camille having prejudiced his parents against him, his predicament was aggravated by the fact that she was expecting a child. Luckily Bazille came to the rescue. He was better off than his friends and had already been of material service to them—to Monet in particular—several times. Now he volunteered to buy *Women in the Garden* for 2500 francs, payable at the rate of fifty francs a month. This was as much of his monthly allowance as he could spare, but it was not enough to support Monet and those now dependent on him. Informed of his plight by Bazille, Monet's parents remained intractable and would do nothing for him until he "settled down." In order to live as cheaply as possible he accepted the hospitality of his aunt, Madame Lecadre, at Sainte-Adresse, just up the coast from Le Havre. He had to leave Camille in Paris for the time being and there she gave birth to a son, Jean. Practically penniless, Monet was unable to come and Bazille, as the child's godfather, had to look after everything.

Women in the Garden was rejected at the 1867 Salon, and though his *Ships rounding the Breakwater at Le Havre* was accepted, it was relegated to the back rooms of the Salon. He remained at Sainte-Adresse all summer, working without a break. "I've got plenty of work cut out for myself," he wrote to Bazille. "I've got twenty canvases or more on the stocks, some stunning seascapes, some figure pieces, some garden scenes."

From this letter we may infer that the *Woman in a Garden* (Hermitage, Leningrad) dates from the summer of 1867. This work, akin to the *Terrace near Le Havre*, has none of the latter's dryness and better conveys the sultriness of mid-summer, with sun and shadows dancing in the foliage of a garden in full flower. The seascapes and views of the beach painted that summer at Sainte-Adresse (many include figures) are based on contrasts of elliptical patches of light and shadow that reconcile Manet's practice with the methods of Boudin and Jongkind.

THE MAGPIE, C. 1869. OWNED BY THE SOCIÉTÉ GUERLAIN, PARIS.

This, Monet's finest snowscape, is variously dated from 1869 to 1872. Much favored by the Japanese and the Dutch and Flemish masters, the theme of landscape under snow was taken up again by Jongkind and Courbet in the mid-19th century and systematically developed thereafter by the Impressionists. Their careful study of the effects of sunlight on snow (paralleling their study of sunlight on water) led them to discover, empirically, the fact that shadows too are charged with color. The whiteness of new-fallen snow provided an ideal ground for subtle variations of color (note here the lovely tints of yellow and blue); of all the Impressionists Sisley was perhaps most adept at this. Monet's first snow pictures go back to 1865; he made many more in the years around 1870, especially when in England, and again around 1880 at Vétheuil. It is not known where this *Magpie* was painted.

STILL LIFE, C. 1869. COLLECTION OF MRS VINCENT ASTOR.

As a young painter, before devoting himself almost exclusively to landscape and open-air painting, Monet tried his hand at many different subjects and genres. Still lifes figure prominently in the work of his prentice years, from 1859 to 1862. One was submitted in 1859 to the Municipal Council of Le Havre to justify his application for a grant; another, thoroughly realistic in treatment, was solicited by his cousin Toulmouche, as a token of his abilities, when Monet applied to him for advice in 1862. Dating from the years 1869-1870 is a little known series of still lifes, much more mature in manner; we reproduce here two of the finest examples.

The revival of interest in the still life around 1870 (it bulks large in the work of Manet and Cézanne at that period) can be set down in part to the persistent influence of the Dutch masters, with their unrivaled genius for this type of painting, and above all to the decisive revelation of Chardin. The famous La Caze donation to the Louvre in 1869 included, significantly enough, twelve still lifes by Chardin. Note the very tangible evolution of technique between the still life with fruit on the opposite page, still traditional in arrangement, with its neutral background, and the *Fish* reproduced below, with its broader technique and freer presentation. The white cloth on the table provides an ideal ground, just as snow does in his contemporary landscapes, for bringing out the subtlest variations of light and color. Monet produced another important series of still lifes in 1880-1882.

FISH, C. 1870. COURTESY OF THE FOGG ART MUSEUM, HARVARD UNIVERSITY.

In the winter of 1867-1868 Monet left his aunt's home at Sainte-Adresse to rejoin Camille and Jean. Again his finances were at a very low ebb and his letters to Bazille show how despondent he was. Then Arsène Houssaye bought his *Woman in a Green Dress* for 800 francs and he was commissioned to make the portrait of Madame Gaudibert of Le Havre. After being turned out of an inn at Fécamp in June 1868, Monet made a—fortunately unsuccessful—attempt on his own life. Assistance from Monsieur Gaudibert enabled him to spend a quiet summer at Fécamp, as is shown by a letter to Bazille.

"I'm surrounded here by all that I love best. I spend my time out of doors, roaming the beaches in rough weather, or watching the fishing smacks go out to sea. Or I tramp the countryside, which is so lovely here that I find it almost more to my liking in winter than in summer. And of course all this time I'm hard at work and I think that this year I'll turn out some worthwhile things... Thanks to this gentleman of Le Havre who's been helping me out, I'm enjoying the most perfect peace and quiet. What I'd love to do is stay forever, just like this, in some quiet spot in the country. I must admit that I don't envy your being in Paris."

Monet remained at Fécamp throughout the autumn and did not return to Paris till the winter of 1869. He then became a frequent visitor to the Café Guerbois, headquarters of Manet and his circle. "It wasn't till 1869 that I saw Manet again," wrote Monet later, "but we became close friends at once, as soon as we met. He invited me to come and see him each evening in a café in the Batignolles district where he and his friends met when the day's work was over. There I met Fantin-Latour and Cézanne, Degas, the art critic Duranty, Emile Zola and several others too. I myself introduced Sisley, Bazille and Renoir. Nothing was more interesting than the talks we had, with their perpetual clashes of opinion. Your mind was held in suspense all the time, you spurred the others on to sincere, disinterested inquiry and were spurred on yourself, you laid in a stock of enthusiasm that kept you going for weeks and weeks until you could give final form to the idea you had in mind. You always went home afterwards better steeled for the fray, with a new sense of purpose and a clearer head."

TWO WOMEN ON THE BEACH AT TROUVILLE, 1870.
MICHEL MONET COLLECTION, SOREL-MOUSSEL.

The famous restaurant and bathing spot on the banks of the Seine known as La Grenouillère (the "froggery"), which served as the setting for some of Maupassant's most acrid stories, were painted from a more cheerful angle by Renoir and Monet, who worked there side by side in August 1869. At least three versions by each artist are extant: the first pictures in which they succeed in rendering the effects of flashing sunlight on moving water by means of small separate strokes of pure color. Bolder, more strongly contrasted than Renoir's, Monet's execution prefigures Impressionism.

LA GRENOUILLÈRE, 1869. COURTESY OF THE METROPOLITAN MUSEUM OF ART, NEW YORK, THE H. O. HAVEMEYER COLLECTION, 1929.

His failure at the 1869 Salon damped the enthusiasm of the few collectors who had shown any interest in him, and again Monet had all he could do to make ends meet. Thanks to Monsieur Gaudibert, however, he was able to settle at Bougival and from this period dates the great friendship between Renoir and Monet. Daily they worked side by side on the banks of the Seine, and in spite of money worries they made their magnificent pictures of La Grenouillère, a popular bathing spot. Painted in delicate shades of green, Renoir's canvases were a tissue of misty transparencies, while Monet's were built up around a hard core of bold contrasts. Patches of bright color jostle one another without any transitions or fusions. One thing they do have in common, however: glints of light on the water are rendered in horizontal, distinctly separate touches —here in embryo is the impressionist brushstroke. Elsewhere in the picture Renoir smoothly blended his brushstrokes; Monet played his off against each other in strong contrasts. But both paid particular attention to the rendering of glints and gleams of light, which are given a large place in these compositions.

When the jury met for the 1870 Salon, Daubigny pleaded Monet's cause but his intervention only antagonized the other jury members; they rejected Monet's entries en bloc and Daubigny resigned in protest. In June Monet and Camille were married but his family refused to receive them. They spent the summer at Trouville, where he found a holiday atmosphere conducive to his work, as can be seen from the seascapes and beach scenes dating from the summer of 1870.

The *Pier at Low Tide* (Budapest), with its radically simplified planes of flat color, inevitably brings Manet to mind; the pictures of women on the beach and the views of the Hôtel des Roches Noires also point, though less directly, to Manet's influence. It was under this impact that Monet gradually

HOTEL DES ROCHES NOIRES, TROUVILLE, 1870.
J. LAROCHE COLLECTION, PARIS.

abandoned his early impasto—legacy of Courbet and the Barbizon painters—in favor of a thinner, more schematic handling of his medium. Characteristic of this evolution, the *Hôtel des Roches Noires* shows that Monet was more of an open-air painter than Manet was, and that he already possessed an incomparable mastery of atmospheric effects. There was a fundamental difference of temperament and sensibility between the two men: Manet was a city-dweller who occasionally found his way to the country, Monet a countryman who occasionally visited the city. Monet had managed, moreover, to a far greater degree than Manet, to disengage his vision from the conventions of the past. Unconsciously or in spite of himself, Manet remained dependent on his reminiscences of the Old Masters and on the traditional notion of values as opposed to color. Monet, when painting from nature, resolutely put out of his mind everything he *knew* and painted only what he *saw*. He dismissed whatever knowledge he had of the object before him and rendered, as simply and directly as he could, the colors that met his eye.

ARGENTEUIL AND IMPRESSIONISM

LONDON - ZAANDAM

THE outbreak of the Franco-Prussian War (July 18, 1870) found Monet at Le Havre, where he remained as that fateful summer wore on. On September 2 came the German breakthrough at Sedan; Napoleon III capitulated and on September 4 the Third Republic was proclaimed.

Leaving Camille and little Jean in Normandy, Monet sailed for England in September. Bazille volunteered for the Zouaves and joined a line regiment in August (he was killed in action at Beaune-la-Rolande on November 28). Manet, as a confirmed republican, waited for the Empire to collapse and then enlisted (as did Degas) in an artillery unit of the National Guard. Pissarro, living at Louveciennes, found himself in the path of the advancing Germans and fled to England, leaving behind hundreds of his pictures together with many that Monet had stored with him. Torn from their frames and used as floor-mats and aprons by the Prussian soldiery, who turned his house into the regimental butchershop, all were destroyed—an irreparable loss, depriving us of by far the greater part of Pissarro's pre-1870 output and a substantial part of Monet's. To these losses, in the case of Monet, must be added the many canvases which he himself ripped to shreds in fits of despair or to prevent their being seized by his creditors.

Things went no better for him in London than in France. The English public showed complete indifference to his work. He submitted some pictures to an exhibition at the Royal Academy, but they were rejected. He had the good luck, however, to run into Daubigny, who introduced him to his own dealer, Paul Durand-Ruel, also a refugee in London, who had opened a gallery at 158 Bond Street. This meeting was providential not only for Monet but also for Pissarro, who met

VIEW OF WESTMINSTER BRIDGE AND THE HOUSES OF PARLIAMENT, 1871.
COLLECTION OF THE RT. HON. JOHN J. ASTOR, LONDON.

Durand-Ruel at the same time. "Without him we'd have starved to death in London," he wrote later. But in spite of his enthusiasm for their work and his persistence in bringing it to public notice, Durand-Ruel failed to sell a single one of their pictures in England. He nevertheless went on buying canvases from Monet and Pissarro, and thus enabled them to keep afloat.

Monet made several views of the Thames in addition to some studies in Hyde Park in which the figures are very roughly silhouetted against a simplified landscape composed of broad, flat planes of color. Pissarro tells of their visits to the museums and how much they were impressed by the English landscape painters, by Constable and Turner in particular. Monet later denied that he had been influenced by Turner at that time, and indeed it is only in the much later series of fog effects on the Thames (1904) that Turner's influence becomes apparent.

In the summer of 1871 Monet left England for Holland, where he painted some landscapes in which the mighty forms of windmills, outlined against the immensity of the sky above the canals in the foreground, are treated in a free, sparkling style very much like that of his Trouville seascapes of 1870.

Life had gone back to normal in Paris now and artists were returning to their old haunts. The group that had formed around Manet in the late sixties now formed again, but this time it centered on Monet. Even before his military service, as early as 1859, Monet had met Pissarro at the Académie Suisse; after his discharge from the army, at Gleyre's studio in 1862, he had met Renoir, Bazille and Sisley. Monet thus formed the link between the group at Gleyre's and the group at the Académie Suisse, where Pissarro had been joined by Cézanne and Guillaumin.

In December 1871 Monet settled at Argenteuil, on the western outskirts of Paris. After a visit to Le Havre in the spring of 1872, he left for Holland, eager to rework a vein that had proved so fruitful in the previous year. It is difficult to distinguish between the pictures made during these two stays in Holland, few of them being dated. Assignable to 1872, however, are those which foreshadow the fully developed technique of his Argenteuil period, those, in other words, in which we find a breaking-up of color into a patchwork of small brushstrokes and a new emphasis on atmospheric vibration.

In the autumn of 1872 Monet returned to Argenteuil where he lived for the next six years, with occasional expeditions to Paris, as is proved by two views of the Boulevard des

Capucines in winter. He saw much of Renoir and they often worked together on the Seine banks. Monet's first river scenes, in 1872-1873, were still built up in separate, unblended strokes and patches of color. A good example is *Pleasure Boats* which, enclosed in a triple frame with a Sisley and a Pissarro, forms a triptych bequeathed to the Louvre by Monsieur May.

During the winter of 1873-1874, again in desperate financial straits, Monet reverted to his old idea of a group exhibition. It seemed indeed to be their last hope, as business was going badly for Durand-Ruel; he was on the verge of bankruptcy

WINDMILLS IN HOLLAND, 1871.
COLLECTION GUY M. BJORKMAN, NEW YORK.

IMPRESSION, SUNRISE, 1872. MUSÉE MARMOTTAN, PARIS.

and had had to suspend his purchases. Pissarro, Cézanne, Renoir, Sisley, Guillaumin, Degas and Berthe Morisot had always been in favor of the plan, and they now made common cause with Monet. The photographer Nadar, who was just then leaving on holiday, very kindly put his studios at their disposal free of charge. Manet was invited to take part but he refused; though entirely in sympathy with them, he was inflexible in his determination to safeguard his independence and, in spite of his rebuffs at the Salon, was convinced that it offered the surest means of catching the public eye.

Their first group exhibition took place in April and May 1874. It created something of a sensation but, as is well known, drew down a hail of derision and abuse from the press and the public at large. The art critic of *Le Charivari*, poking fun at a canvas by Monet entitled *Impression, Sunrise*, coined the word "Impressionism" as a gibe at the group. Monet adopted the name at once and launched it on its glorious career; from now on he was the acknowledged "ringleader" of the new school of painting.

But this *succès de scandale* did little to improve their fortunes. Evicted by his landlord, Monet hardly knew which way to turn, when luckily Manet came to the rescue and found him another house at Argenteuil. Manet's family had owned property for several generations at Gennevilliers, across the Seine from Argenteuil, and he knew the neighborhood well. One of his friends there was Gustave Caillebotte, a ship designer and amateur painter. Manet's abstention from the group exhibition thus by no means estranged him from Monet, and the two men worked together for most of the summer, Manet painting the most airy, light-filled pictures he had yet produced. Renoir often came out from Paris and Caillebotte too often joined them.

That brief summer of 1874 at Argenteuil is a landmark in the history of painting. A particularly fertile period for all, it cemented a unity of outlook and endeavor between them which lasted, however, no more than the space of that summer; thereafter each went his own way.

Monet worked out of doors from morning to night with the singlemindedness of a seeker who feels his prize within arm's reach. In order to paint on the river he fitted up a small

This is an unusual canvas in Monet's output. The rhythmic pattern of the coalmen, dark silhouettes moving on long planks between the barges and the river bank, strikes a contrast with the sauntering passer-bys on the bridge above. A bleak winter day and the indistinctness of the figures, all seen against the light, heighten the dramatic character of a strongly linear composition. The stress and tension here implied by physical effort is almost totally absent from Impressionism—a leisurely art of dreamy or lyrical surrender to the joy of life and beauties of nature.

MEN UNLOADING COAL, 1872.
PIERRE DURAND-RUEL COLLECTION, PARIS.

boat with a forward cabin where he could store his painting tackle and take shelter in bad weather. In this Caillebotte no doubt gave him professional advice and assistance. A canvas awning was stretched from the cabin to the stern to protect him from the sun and there he usually set up his easel. Thus we see him in Manet's picture in Munich: *Claude Monet painting on his Boat*.

Working in his boat on the Seine, Monet not only registered the most fleeting effects of sunset and sunrise, but was able to choose the angle of vision that suited him best. It was in these circumstances that he produced his magnificent series of *Regattas*, which established his position as an unrivaled painter of the most transient effects of atmospheric light. His technique evolved accordingly: he broke up masses and, in his eagerness to render gleams of sunlight on rippling water, he came to apply his paints in small, distinct, comma-like brushstrokes that broke up surfaces into a thousand fragments. In time, as he sought to render atmospheric vibration as a whole, he extended this technique to the entire canvas. But it was neither a sudden nor a continuous development, and in Monet's output at Argenteuil from 1873 to 1875 there are canvases executed in broad, blended brushstrokes as well as in small, distinct touches; there are also very many combining both techniques.

The *Sailboat moored to a Landing-stage* (Durand-Ruel Collection)—of which Renoir, working alongside Monet, made a companion picture (Portland), just as he did of *The Duck Pond*—has light effects much like those in *Argenteuil Bridge* (Personnaz Collection, Louvre), dated 1874. But instead of being painted in the small separate brushstrokes that make the latter canvas rough and granular to the touch, it is so smoothly, broadly handled that it is generally given an earlier date, though the colors are much more blended and vibrant than those of *Pleasure Boats* (May Collection, Louvre).

Monet 19

—

ARGENTEUIL BRIDGE, 1874. LOUVRE, PARIS.

A picturesque riverside village a few miles west of Paris and a popular
resort of boating enthusiasts and holiday-makers, Argenteuil has become
synonymous with Impressionism at its prime, in the mid-seventies, when
Monet's best friends, including Manet himself who lived nearby at Gennevilliers, joined him there almost daily in summertime and vied with him in
friendly rivalry. A new style of painting came into existence which, by
means of pure, unmixed colors applied to the canvas in distinct, unblended
strokes, suggests the brightness of the sun and the glitter of light with
a fresh and natural vivacity which had never before been seen in painting.

THE RAILWAY BRIDGE AT ARGENTEUIL, C. 1873. LOUVRE, PARIS.

The metal railway bridge over the Seine constitutes the "backbone" of several masterpieces of the Argenteuil period, and forms the solid axis on which the weltering reflections of sky and water shift and flicker. Usually cut short by the picture frame (in the Japanese manner), the metal span of the bridge rests on a series of twin piers and either traverses the picture space lengthwise or (as here) at an oblique angle. A passing train sends up a lazily curling billow of smoke against the tenuous cloud-rack of the summer sky. Clumps of bushes on the river bank climb steeply in the foreground to the level of the bridge and partly screen it from view.

59

In the series of *Regattas*, painted from his boat, slight stylistic differences are discernible from picture to picture. These reveal a rather subtle line of evolution, but a significant one.

Sailboat at Argenteuil (Bravington Collection), tacking with all sails set across the Seine, represents the next step after *Pleasure Boats* (May Collection). It is handled like the latter, with the paint swept on broadly in thin coats, but the strokes of the brush are no longer quite so separate and distinct as they are in *Pleasure Boats*; instead of being juxtaposed and contrasting with each other, planes tend to fuse and intermingle. *Regatta in Fine Weather* (Caillebotte Collection, Louvre) marks a further stage. Reflections on the water are no longer rendered in molten

REGATTA IN GRAY WEATHER, 1874. LOUVRE, PARIS.

dabs of color, but in straight, horizontal, distinctly separate brushstrokes. These strokes, however, are larger than those in *Regatta in Gray Weather* (Camondo Collection, Louvre). Here, in order to render choppy water ruffled by the wind, Monet dabbed on his paints in small, flickering touches that convey an effect of movement and agitation, and though motivated by circumstances (i.e. the state of the weather) they nevertheless mark a further step in his increasing concern with effects of atmospheric vibration.

In each of these pictures he never failed to adapt his technique to the nature of the scene before him. Sky, water, trees, sails, houses, no two of these things are treated in the same way. The brushstroke is adjusted in every case to the visual impression, which in turn depends not only on light conditions but on the form and texture of the object or element in question.

During the summer Monet was so completely engrossed in nautical subjects that he apparently found time for only one rural landscape: *Springtime* (Berlin), a masterpiece of sunny airiness, painted with the utmost simplicity in flat colors. At the approach of winter his thoughts turned again to the open country and he made some snowscapes, mostly handled in thin coats of modulated color (for example, *Train in the Snow*, Musée Marmottan, Paris, dated 1875), sometimes in a thick impasto, but always smoothly brushed on, without any division of color.

As a result of the severe winters of the early seventies (borne out by his snowscapes), Monet felt the pinch more than ever and, to make things worse, there seemed to be no prospect of better times ahead, for the "incomprehensible" novelty of his painting only widened the breach between him and the public. With his stout physique Monet could bear the hardships of cold and hunger, but his wife's frail health was permanently injured. His painter friends were Monet's only resource, but the whole group was faring badly.

SPRINGTIME, 1874. STAATSGEMÄLDESAMMLUNGEN, BERLIN-DAHLEM.

Renoir then proposed that, instead of a second exhibition, they should hold an auction sale at the Hôtel Drouot. The idea seemed a good one and was adopted. The sale took place on March 20, 1875, but in an uproarious atmosphere of hostility and intrigue, and they made little out of it. Seventy-five works by Sisley, Monet, Renoir and Berthe Morisot fetched a total of

14,491 francs, but this included many repurchases by the artists themselves. Monet put up twenty canvases which went for 4,290 francs; the prices paid per canvas varied from 160 to 325 francs. *Paris-Journal* thus described the sale: "Much entertainment was provided by the violet countrysides, red rivers, black streams, green and yellow women and blue children which the pundits of the new school held up to the public admiration."

WILD POPPIES, 1873. LOUVRE, PARIS.

BREAKFAST IN THE GARDEN, 1872. LOUVRE, PARIS.

This, the last of Monet's early large-scale compositions, comprises several motifs treated turn by turn. A teapot and fruit stand on a white tablecloth, spread on a table in the flower garden behind the house. Jean, the artist's firstborn son, is playing on the ground beside the table. Two young ladies in bright dresses stand in front of the house, looking into the garden. A straw hat with long black ribbons dangles from the branches of the tree. This charming work, "intimism in the open air," is the prototype of many such scenes painted several decades later by Bonnard and Vuillard.

In his Argenteuil period, when not painting on the river, Monet confined himself to intimate garden scenes redolent of summer holidays in the suburbs of Paris; only later did he range into the open countryside. Young ladies in those days seldom ventured out of doors in summertime without a parasol whose colors matched those of their dress. Monet made the most of this gracious accessory (first painted by Courbet), which diffuses light and casts shadows and reflections on faces. This elegant stroller in the privacy of her garden pauses beside a bed of gladioli, whose blossoms give Monet an opportunity of demonstrating the wealth of the new impressionist palette. The division of color intensifies the vibration of the atmosphere.

GLADIOLI, C. 1873. DETROIT INSTITUTE OF ARTS COLLECTION.

The sale brought one tangible asset: a new buyer in the person of Victor Chocquet. An official in the customs administration, not a rich man by any means but a fervent, disinterested art lover, Chocquet joined the small, select band of the group's early admirers and collectors.

Several views of the Seine at Argenteuil with sailboats riding at anchor, dated 1875, are treated in the same vein as those of the previous year (Personnaz Collection, Louvre, and Rhode Island School of Design, Providence). This was not, however, so productive a summer as that of 1874; Monet was harassed by money worries and anxiety about his wife's health. In the autumn he appealed to Dr de Bellio and Emile Zola. On the verge several times of being evicted and dispossessed, he was only saved by the generous help of his friends.

Money had to be raised somehow and the group decided to organize a second exhibition in April 1876, this time in Durand-Ruel's gallery in the Rue Le Peletier. Monet showed eighteen canvases, including several views of the bridge and the Seine at Argenteuil and a portrait of his wife, *Camille in a Japanese Dress*; the latter was not unfavorably received and he had the good luck to sell it for 2,000 francs. The official critics, needless to say, reviewed the exhibition with their usual patronizing disdain. An article by Albert Wolff in the *Figaro* began as follows: "The Rue Le Peletier is an unlucky street. After the fire at the Opera House, it is now the scene of another disaster. I refer to the exhibition, said to be of painting, which has just opened at Durand-Ruel's."

Ernest Hoschedé, a financier and collector who had already bought some of his canvases, invited Monet to spend the summer of 1876 with him and his wife at their country home, the Château de Montgeron (Seine-et-Oise), where he was able

THE RUE MONTORGUEIL DECKED OUT WITH FLAGS, 1878. MUSÉE DE ROUEN. ▶

GARE SAINT-LAZARE, 1877.
COURTESY OF THE FOGG ART MUSEUM, HARVARD UNIVERSITY.

to work under ideal conditions without worrying where his next meal was to come from. Among his Montgeron pictures, in addition to some garden landscapes and an autumn hunting scene, was *White Turkeys* (Polignac Collection, Louvre). Though it was obviously executed in summertime (as the leafage of the trees proves) and exhibited early in April 1877, this picture is dated 1877; we can only suppose that, having painted it in the summer of 1876, Monet for some reason post-dated it when the time came to exhibit the painting.

In spite of the almost apostolic zeal displayed by Chocquet in bringing visitors to the show and trying to convert them,

ST. LAZARE STATION, 1878.
PRIVATE AMERICAN COLLECTION.

the third group exhibition fared no better than the previous ones. For Monet the year 1877 is notable chiefly for his Gare Saint-Lazare series, begun in 1876 and continued well into 1878. Painted for the most part in a rich impasto consisting, apparently, of a multitude of small brushstrokes sufficiently blended to be indistinguishable from one another, this series is a landmark in his career. While these views of a great railway station show that Monet had a sharp eye for the poetic side of city life in his day, they also prove, even more strikingly, that the subject itself was only of secondary importance to him. No doubt he gives us a faithful picture of a contemporary scene, but this was only incidental to his true purpose: the rendering of light as it played in and out of whirling clouds of smoke thrown up by locomotives. As always Monet regarded the object itself with a detachment verging on indifference; he was concerned only with the visual sensations it gave rise to.

At least four of these views date from 1877: the *Pont de l'Europe* (Musée Marmottan, Paris), in which the smoke gives a bluish tinge to light; the *Normandy Train coming in* (Art Institute of Chicago), of which there exists a very similar but undated version; two views of the main hall of the station, both painted from the same spot on the departure platform, one (Wertheim Collection, Fogg Art Museum) bathed in a cool, blue-grey light, while in the other (Louvre) fleecy patches of blue sky are played off against billowing smoke. The juxtaposition of warm and cool patches brings to mind Leonardo da Vinci's remark, to the effect that the same cloud of smoke appears brown or blue depending on whether it is seen against a background darker or lighter than itself.

FROM VÉTHEUIL TO GIVERNY

POURVILLE - ETRETAT - BORDIGHERA - BELLE-ILE

For all the interest he took in painting various aspects of Paris, notably the Tuileries, Monet never felt at home in the city and left suburban Argenteuil in 1878 for the country village of Vétheuil, on the Seine about midway between Paris and Rouen. But another trial was in store for him there. After the birth of his second son in March 1878, his wife's health declined and she died in October 1879. Monet remained at Vétheuil till 1881. During those four years, in spite of his bereavement, his poverty, his anxiety for his children, he carried on with his work, persisting in his chosen path, reverting again and again to the same motifs seen in different seasons, at different times of day: the road through the village, the village itself seen from the opposite bank of the Seine or from the bend of the river with a hillside in the background. The severity of the winters gave him an opportunity of painting snow effects and views of the ice on the Seine.

His Vétheuil period confirmed the trend of his art (already clearly marked in his Argenteuil pictures) toward the expression of atmospheric light. But now, as he concentrated less on nautical themes and more on straight landscape, his subject matter sometimes encouraged him to use a full brush, with the result that some of his snowscapes are overpainted and ponderous. In most of his summer landscapes, on the other hand, and in many winter ones too, he broke up masses more and more boldly into a checkerwork of separate brushstrokes. These landscapes are characterized by a horizontal composition.

Winter in Vétheuil (Buffalo) is a typical example of the playing off of snow against rich brown earth, while *Entrance to the Village of Vétheuil* (Boston) is pervaded by a bluish tonality that gives it an airy, weightless luminosity. The views of drift-ice

WINTER IN VÉTHEUIL, 1878. ALBRIGHT ART GALLERY,
BUFFALO, NEW YORK.

on the Seine also vary greatly in their effects, running from the most aerial to the most massive. The different ways in which icicles and water reflect and refract light gave rise to contrasts and alternations that must have delighted Monet. It was this very problem that he tackled twenty years later at Giverny when he painted water lilies.

In 1878, at the news that his friend and benefactor Ernest Hoschedé was utterly ruined, Monet at once came forward and took Madame Hoschedé and her six children into his own home. He thus paid an old debt of gratitude but his resources were strained to the limit. He was entirely dependent on advances from Durand-Ruel, whose business affairs, fortunately, had taken a turn for the better. In December 1881 he moved from Vétheuil to Poissy, near Saint-Germain-en-Laye. But finding the place uninspiring, he spent the rest of the winter on the Channel coast, first at Dieppe, then at Pourville, "a delightful spot in the neighborhood of Dieppe"; there he stayed over

ENTRANCE TO THE VILLAGE OF VÉTHEUIL: SNOW, 1879.
COLLECTION MUSEUM OF FINE ARTS, BOSTON.

two months, availing himself of splendid weather "to work like a madman." But when he returned to Poissy in May the spell was broken: "illness has entered the house like a fateful visitant" and he had all he could do to look after his numerous charges.

Bound and determined to leave Poissy, he finally went back to Pourville in June 1882, taking Madame Hoschedé and the children with him. But by now the weather had turned bad and his work went poorly. The letters he wrote to Durand-Ruel in the course of that summer show him fluctuating between moods of hope and despair, till finally, on September 26, he wrote as follows: "This season, to put it bluntly, has been a dead loss for me and I might as well resign myself to the fact. I won't say that all these difficulties may not have compelled me to exert myself, and even to progress, but there is nothing to show for it as yet, for I don't see a single piece of good work in all these half-finished canvases. I feel very unhappy and worried about it all."

The canvases referred to are those painted on the cliffs in the neighborhood of Dieppe, Pourville and Varengeville. Almost all present the same characteristics: a composition in the Japanese manner with a plunging glimpse of the sea viewed from a foreground of cliffs; a dazzling flood of light that seems to volatilize everything; a technique of small, "comma" brush-strokes calculated to render these flashing particles of light.

Cliffs at Dieppe (Stockholm, Zurich), *Custom House* (Phila-delphia, Newark and Ansley Collection), *Fishermen's Cottages at Varengeville* (Boston, Rotterdam), all exemplify this particular stage of Monet's work in which, more searchingly than at any other time of his career, he boldly dislocated masses under the impact of bright sunlight, whose glitter and vibrancy he ren-dered by means of small, separate brushstrokes of pure color. But even then he never worked systematically. We need only inspect these canvases from close at hand to see how greatly the technique varies. While the grass of a meadow, for example, is seen to consist of a mass of tiny flicks of the brush, the sea, on the contrary, is rendered in sweeping streaks. Sky and clouds are handled in still another manner. Always Monet follows the promptings of his sensibility, never holding to a preconceived system. And when weather conditions forced him to change his customary motifs for others and momentarily to abandon those vistas over the sea, Monet instinctively changed his technique to meet the case. This is shown by several versions of *Cliffs at Pourville*, viewed from the beach at low tide in gray weather and dating from this same year, 1882. Tiny, flickering strokes have given place to masses of full-bodied color which express the sensation of ponderous immobility conveyed by tall cliffs under an overcast sky. Yet this change of technique under changed lighting conditions did not prevent him from

ETRETAT, 1883. LOUVRE, PARIS.

rendering with inspired truthfulness and subtlety the semi-transparent, semi-reflective texture of the large pools of sea-water left on the beach in the foreground at low tide. He showed the same versatility in the pictures painted in the following years at Etretat and Belle-Ile, in the South of France and in the Creuse department.

Monet spent the autumn of 1882 at Poissy, where he went through the great flood of that year. "I'm no longer a painter just now," he wrote to Durand-Ruel, "but a rescue-worker, a boatman, a furniture remover." In January 1883 he returned to Normandy, working out of doors at Etretat despite stormy weather. Then in April he left Poissy for good and settled —together with the Hoschedé family which he had practically adopted—at Giverny, near Vernon, on the banks of the Epte, a tributary of the Seine. The expenses of moving and furnishing a new house obliged him to appeal to Durand-Ruel time and again for advances, and these constant money worries hampered his work. But after a period of adjustment he felt at home again and spent all summer at Giverny.

In December 1883 Monet and Renoir made a brief trip together to the Riviera, and Monet was delighted with the Mediterranean. Hardly had he returned to Giverny when he decided to go south again on a painting expedition, but alone this time, preferring not to expose himself to the powerful influence of his friend's art. This concern for safeguarding the purity of his vision was characteristic of Monet, and increased as he grew older. Of the works he did on the Riviera he wrote to Durand-Ruel: "Perhaps they will raise a bit of a cry from the enemies of blue and pink, for it is precisely the vividness and magic of the sunlight here that I have sought to render. Those who have never seen this region or have seen it with only half an eye will, I feel sure, accuse me of exaggeration, even though my tones are still pitched too low..."

The pictures referred to are in themselves sufficient proof of the open-mindedness and receptivity to which these lines testify. Monet had a prodigious faculty of surrendering himself to the visual sensations induced by the scene before his eyes, and of recreating an exact pictorial equivalent of that scene. If some of the canvases he painted in Normandy seem hard and chalky, that is due to the nature of the country itself and to the fidelity with which he recorded his impression of it. When at other times, in other places, he sets to work on a bright-colored motif, he responds to those colors immediately and in exact proportion to their intensity. Never did he distort what he saw for arbitrary reasons, or misrepresent his sensations in compliance with any preconceived idea.

During a two-month stay at Etretat in the autumn of 1885 he painted a series of views of the coastline and sea. Blue and mauve effects of light on the chalk cliffs are played off against the blues and greens of the water with serene power and truthfulness. Fishing boats stranded on the beach, for example *Boats in Winter Quarters* (Chicago), offered an ideal pretext for bright colors in a very different vein, suggestive of Fauvism nearly twenty years before that movement began.

In 1886 Durand-Ruel sailed for New York in hopes of opening up an American market for his large stock of impressionist paintings. Monet took a gloomy view of those hopes and, seeing his only source of income cut off for the time being, bitterly reproached his old dealer for abandoning him. In order to support himself and his family he now began selling his work to the Galerie Petit, and this put a strain on his relations with Durand-Ruel.

At Belle-Ile, in the late summer and autumn of 1886, he reverted to the theme of cliff and sea which had been so successful at Etretat. But he was in Brittany now, and the texture and coloring of the cliffs did not lend themselves to the same

THE ROCK ARCH, ETRETAT, 1886. DURAND-RUEL COLLECTION, PARIS.

BORDIGHERA, 1884. ART INSTITUTE OF CHICAGO.

His enthusiasm aroused by a first brief excursion to the south with Renoir in December 1883, Monet went back alone in January 1884 and worked for three months on the Riviera, first at Bordighera, then at Menton. Always sensitive to the specific atmosphere and character of a given place, he at once found expression for the almost tropical splendors he saw around him. The swaying rhythms of exuberant vegetation magnify the vibrancy of the atmosphere. Through a tangle of pines we get a glimpse of the Mediterranean and the white houses of the town huddled in the sun.

treatment. Instead of reflecting light, as the smooth, white chalk cliffs of Normandy had done, the rough dark granite of the Breton coast merely formed a massive block of ruddy colors.

Here again Monet handled color boldly, but always so appropriately to the scene before him as to refute the charge sometimes brought against him of overdoing the brightness of his colors. The vigorous canvases executed at Cap-Martin, Antibes and Juan-les-Pins in 1888 are typical of this chromatic accuracy, while a fresh example of the perfect objectivity of his vision is provided in the following year by the landscapes painted in the Creuse department of west-central France; these differ markedly in tonality and aspect from both his Riviera and his Normandy landscapes, just because they so very accurately render the specific character of the Creuse region.

Although these expeditions kept him away from home for months on end, he worked each year at Giverny in the intervals. In 1892 Monet and Madame Hoschedé were married and thereafter he seldom left Giverny. Durand-Ruel had been successful in his American venture and the increasing demand for impressionist paintings had at last secured Monet a comfortable income. He now bought the house in which he lived at Giverny and arranged it to suit himself.

In 1890-1891 he began his series of *Poplars* and *Haystacks*, seen at different seasons. He thoroughly explored the possibilities of a single motif and made it yield a full crop of paintings as numerous and varied as the lighting in which they were made. First he settled on a basic compositional scheme: a winding line of poplars along the banks of the Epte, rising at right angles to the horizontal ground-line. He then tested out several viewpoints, finally adopting an angle of vision that happily combined a spiral with verticals and horizontals. With his motif thus defined, he painted it day by day, season by season, in every possible light.

In 1890, after a decade of restless journeying up and down the Seine valley
and the Channel coast, Monet settled for good at Giverny, about midway
between Paris and Rouen. In December, thanks to the increasing demand
for his pictures, he was able to buy the house he had been renting there.
Between the *Poplars* and *Haystacks* came a few canvases representing fields
of oats and meadows. No painter has ever been more sensitive to the
"anatomy" of time and place; none has more feelingly evoked the sweep
and respiration of space, the drift of clouds, the secret heartbeat of nature.

FIELD OF OATS, 1890.
COLLECTION OF MR AND MRS OGDEN PHIPPS.

Mc

POPLARS AT GIVERNY: SUNRISE, 1888.
COLLECTION OF MR WILLIAM B. JAFFE, NEW YORK.

Monet was just as scrupulous about the linear structure of his composition
as he was about color and light values. The slender trunks of poplars form a
tenuous curtain of waving leafage lit up by the faint pink glow of the rising
sun. The spectator is made aware of their tangible presence and, at the
same time, of their subtle evaporation in the hazy, humid atmosphere of
early morning. In 1890 Monet was so much taken by the theme of poplars
bordering the Epte and their reflections in the river that he painted them
from his boat throughout the spring and summer and well into the autumn.

POPLARS, 1891. COLLECTION OF MADAME LEFÉBURE, PARIS.

The linear stylization foreshadowing the decorative eccentricities of the *art nouveau* of 1900, combined with the rippling mirror of the water, here attains an almost abstract degree of purity. The subtlest gradations of color swirl and interfuse from rectangle to rectangle, above and below a line of purple shrubbery, against evanescent textures of sky and water.

POPLARS, 1891. COURTESY OF THE METROPOLITAN MUSEUM OF ART, NEW YORK.

After the first series of *Poplars* along the banks of the Epte (spring and summer 1890), Monet began the series of *Haystacks* (some 30 of them still exist). He worked at them throughout the autumn and winter, observing them under countless variations of light and weather, even under snow. Fifteen *Haystacks* were exhibited at Durand-Ruel's in May 1891. They met with an instantaneous success; all were sold at prices varying from 3,000 to 4,000 francs. Like a backcloth or reminiscence across many of them runs a curtain of distant poplars. Monet's method was to take several canvases out to the motif and work at them successively. "I'm plugging away," he wrote to Gustave Geffroy on October 7, 1890, "toiling doggedly at a series of different effects (on haystacks), but at this time of year the sun goes down so fast that I can't keep up with it. I'm becoming so slow in my ways, it's maddening. But the further I go, the more I realize the amount of work involved in rendering what I'm after: the 'instantaneous-ness', the envelope of things, with the same light pouring in everywhere. More than ever easy canvases tossed off at one go get my back up."

HAYSTACKS, 1891. PRIVATE COLLECTION, PARIS.

After the *Poplars* and *Haystacks* came the *Cathedrals*, a series devoted to the great Gothic cathedral of Rouen. Monet set to work in March 1892, gave it up for a time, then resumed work in February-March 1893, painting from the window of a room he rented over a shop ("Au Caprice", 81, Rue Grand-Pont). He returned to Giverny in the early spring of 1893 and there, for the rest of the year and most of 1894, worked from memory on the canvases. Hence the thick, well-kneaded impasto suggestive of the actual texture of stone. Twenty of them were exhibited at Durand-Ruel's in May 1895, in a sequence running from dawn to dusk. In an enthusiastic article entitled *La Révolution des Cathédrales*, Clemenceau extolled the

PAGE 91: ROUEN CATHEDRAL, WEST FAÇADE, SUNLIGHT, 1894. ►
NATIONAL GALLERY OF ART, WASHINGTON, D.C. (CHESTER DALE COLLECTION).

PAGE 92: ROUEN CATHEDRAL, THE FAÇADE AT SUNSET, 1894. ►
COLLECTION MUSEUM OF FINE ARTS, BOSTON.

Then came the series of *Haystacks*. For these he adopted an even more methodical procedure. He went out to the motif with a whole batch of canvases on which he painted successively, working at each only for the brief moment that corresponded to a particular light condition.

But it was the series of *Rouen Cathedral* in 1892-1894 that provided the most complete and spectacular demonstration of his methods and his virtuosity in applying them. From the window of a hotel room, chosen for its angle of vision, he recorded the successive aspects of façade and portal in accordance with the changing position of the sun and changes of weather.

A trip to Norway in 1895 gave him an opportunity of tackling new effects of snow, ice and frost. But except for this trip and a few others to Pourville on the Channel coast, Monet confined himself more and more to interpreting familiar scenes in the immediate neighborhood of Giverny. Without serializing them, he reverted again and again to favorite motifs: *Banks of the Seine*, *Banks of the Epte*, *Oatfields*, *Poppies*, *Meadows* curtained off by rows of trees. Never before had this countryside (in the Eure department, midway between Paris and Rouen) found so sensitive an interpreter of its luminous, faintly misted atmosphere. The aerial lightness of a radiant spring morning in that part of France, with lush meadows ruffled by an early breeze, has never been more faithfully rendered than by Monet.

In the late nineties Monet set to work on a new project. Deflecting the course of a stream that flowed into the Epte, he channeled it into the garden behind his house where it formed a pond, which he planted with water lilies. With the poplars that were already there and the willows he planted himself, he soon obtained an exotic water-garden, full of luxuriant plantlife, which he completed with a small bridge in Japanese style. For a time his principal theme, this soon became his almost exclusive source of inspiration.

"symphonic splendor" of the canvases as a group and distinguished four color series (a gray, a white, a blue and an iridescent series) corresponding to four different times of day. They were decried by many of the younger artists, but their technical mastery elicited the unqualified admiration of Cézanne, Degas, Renoir, and Pissarro who, on May 26, wrote as follows to his son Lucien: "It is the work, well thought out, of a man with a will of his own, pursuing every nuance of elusive effects, such as no other artist that I can see has captured. Some deny that there is any necessity for pursuing those effects. Personally I think that the pursuit of any effect is justified when it is heartfelt as this is."

◀ PAGE 89: ROUEN CATHEDRAL AND THE COUR D'ALBANE, EARLY MORNING, 1894. COLLECTION MUSEUM OF FINE ARTS, BOSTON.

◀ PAGE 90: ROUEN CATHEDRAL, THE PORTAL, 1894. COLLECTION OF THE VICOMTESSE DE MONTFORT.

Monet 4

WATERLOO BRIDGE, GRAY DAY, 1903.
NATIONAL GALLERY OF ART, WASHINGTON, D.C. (CHESTER DALE COLLECTION).

He returned to London, however, in the early 1900s and executed a series of fog effects on the Thames which, with their rapturous lyricism, come much closer to Turner than did his London pictures of 1871.

In 1908 he paid his first visit to Venice, whose peculiarly limpid light came like a revelation to him and he wrote to Gustave Geffroy: "What a pity I didn't come here earlier when I was young and bold and would stop at nothing!" But he went boldly to work nonetheless and, stripping their anecdotal and historical associations from the Ducal Palace and the other

WATERLOO BRIDGE, GRAY DAY, 1903.
NATIONAL GALLERY OF ART, WASHINGTON, D.C. (CHESTER DALE COLLECTION).

He returned to London, however, in the early 1900s and executed a series of fog effects on the Thames which, with their rapturous lyricism, come much closer to Turner than did his London pictures of 1871.

In 1908 he paid his first visit to Venice, whose peculiarly limpid light came like a revelation to him and he wrote to Gustave Geffroy: "What a pity I didn't come here earlier when I was young and bold and would stop at nothing!" But he went boldly to work nonetheless and, stripping their anecdotal and historical associations from the Ducal Palace and the other

great *palazzi* of Venice, he painted them in the shining purity of his initial vision of them, glimpsed through a blaze of Mediterranean light.

After 1900, except for these trips to London and Venice, Monet devoted himself entirely to sets of pictures inspired by

THE HOUSES OF PARLIAMENT: THE SUN COMING THROUGH FOG, 1904.
DURAND-RUEL COLLECTION, PARIS.

THE DUCAL PALACE AT VENICE, 1908.
IN THE BROOKLYN MUSEUM COLLECTION.

his water-garden. The first set, begun in 1899, centered on the
arch of the bridge spanning the pond, with clusters of water
lilies underneath and weeping willows all around. There are
undeniable echoes of the *art nouveau* of 1900 in Monet's handling
of these plant forms, though he never adopted the flat tints
and heavy contours of that decorative art. His own approach,

moreover, is distinguished by a narrowing down of the field of vision, unlike anything to be seen in his earlier landscapes.

Indeed, in his next set of pictures, produced between 1905 and 1910, the field of vision is strictly confined to the surface of the water, seen in recession at a low angle. Nothing is visible but floating water lilies and shimmering reflections of the sky.

THE GRAND CANAL, VENICE, 1908.
COLLECTION MUSEUM OF FINE ARTS, BOSTON.

The same holds good for the large-scale canvases painted after 1910, but while the subject is steadily magnified in proportion as the size of the canvas increases, at the same time the area depicted progressively narrows down. The object is seen in close-up, along a more and more vertical line of sight, till finally every suggestion of perspective disappears and the lilies are spread out upon the surface of the water viewed from directly overhead.

Then, about 1915, Monet conceived the idea of a vast decorative ensemble on the theme of water lilies. He had a new studio built especially for this purpose and spent the last ten years of his life carrying out this grandiose project.

Toward the end he suffered from eye trouble and a cataract forced him to stop working for a time in 1922-1923. But even when failing eyesight prevented him from distinguishing objects with precision, Monet went on painting, registering on his canvas the color impressions to which he responded as keenly as ever, and which, now as always, were the be-all and end-all of his life. The object before him, already dislocated by the undulations of its own reflection on the water, now disappeared altogether in an indefinable modulation of colors.

THE WATER LILIES

1900-1926

As soon as they appeared, the *Water Lilies* of Monet's old age, those hymns to light, plant life and water, incurred the displeasure of both the well-wishers and the detractors of Impressionism. The first were baffled by Monet's new manner; the second were blind to the new depth of vision these works revealed. Misunderstood and neglected for over thirty years, the *Water Lilies* are at last receiving the recognition they deserve.

Having had the privilege, from childhood up, of seeing and familiarizing myself with them in the setting at Giverny in which they were created (the *only* setting, let me add, that can do justice to them), it reflects no particular credit on me to say that personally I have never shared that incomprehension. To see the *Water Lilies* in the garden studio especially built to house them was to see them in natural, harmonious conjunction with radiant summer days spent in the garden at Giverny beside the pond which inspired them. It was a delight which those who experienced it will never forget.

I cannot deny that, for me at least, the spell is irremediably broken in the Musée de l'Orangerie, in that bleak back room which, designed especially for the *Water Lilies* in 1925, nevertheless baldly reduces them to a mural decoration—and they are ever so much more than that. The way in which they are encased there, in a long horizontal belt around the concave wall, restricts them to the narrow, perfectly extraneous function of emphasizing the ellipsoidal line of the architecture. Monet himself contributed to this over-modest setting by approving the whole project at the time and by doing his utmost to adapt his panels to it. To break and diversify the even horizontal flow of the paintings around the room, he sprinkled the foreground with willow fronds suggestive of the decorative style of *art*

WATER LILIES, 1899.
MRS ALBERT D. LASKER COLLECTION, NEW YORK.

nouveau, fashionable around 1900. At the same time they introduce a third dimension which strikes an uncalled-for contrast
with the sheer vertical plane of the water surface; the latter,
with its rich play of light effects, was theme enough in itself.

The setting, then, in which the *Water Lilies* have been exhibited to the public in part explains both the eclipse they underwent for over a quarter of a century and the keen revival of interest in them caused by the recent revelation of further *Water Lilies* hitherto hidden from view in the studio at Giverny. The evolution of taste and ideas in the course of the past half-century explains the rest.

This evolution, as far as painting is concerned, began with the dissensions that led to the break-up of the impressionist movement in the eighties. While Monet went on, single-mindedly pursuing the subtlest, most elusive effects and variations of light and atmosphere, Pissarro, Renoir, Cézanne, Van Gogh and Gauguin each branched out in different directions. The Neo-Impressionism of Seurat, with which Pissarro threw in his lot in 1886, was both a logical development of Impressionism and a reaction against it. The systematic, scientific application of the principles which Monet discovered and applied by trial and error signified in effect a tacit condemnation of the intuitive, empirical nature of his art. As for Renoir, after an uneasy interlude in which he toyed with a harshly linear, Ingresque style, he finally reconciled his concern for form with his love of light, fusing both in an inimitable glorification of volume saturated with color. Cézanne, however, always deferring to his "sensations," gradually exacted from them not an atmospheric so much as a geological revelation of the visible world. After a fling at Neo-Impressionism, whose narrow harness failed to hold him long in check, Van Gogh hit his stride at Arles, throwing off every constraint in a jubilant, pre-expressionist exaltation of color and line. But it was the symbolism of Gauguin which worked the most radical transformation of Impressionism. Gauguin sacrificed the visual aspect of things to the expression, in terms of line and color, of the "idea" they engendered in the mind. He rejected outright the whole battery of naturalistic effects calculated to suggest space and light, and adopted flat colors and heavy contour lines.

The upshot of these powerfully diverging currents was Fauvism, which abandoned every semblance of fidelity to outward appearances in favor of a rapturous glorification of color—but color handled more plastically than it was by the slightly later followers of Van Gogh, with their bias toward expressionist distortion. In spite of this reaction, however, Fauvism and Expressionism remained, like Impressionism, essentially dependent on the sensation induced by the object.

This was no longer true of Cubism, which rejected the outer world as it appears to our senses and built up another one out of a select assortment of elements artificially reassembled in the mind. This essentially cerebral art stood at the opposite pole from the essentially sensuous art of Impressionism. No wonder then that the meat of the one was the poison of the other. The rise of Cubism and the era that followed, during which its influence spread and was assimilated, set up a reaction against Impressionism, whose achievement was belittled and whose most characteristic representative, Claude Monet, was disregarded by a whole generation of artists.

The very nature of abstract art might lead us to suppose that it stands at an even further remove from Impressionism than Cubism did. The fact is, however, that by reacting against cubist rationalism and reverting to the basic forms and forces that appeal to the human instinct, abstract art has contributed to focus the attention of the younger generation of painters on the master of Giverny.

The first wave of abstractionism unleashed by Cubism was based, it is true, on a rational, intellectualized system of symbols. But it was followed by a purer form of abstraction embodying a very different conception of art. The latter, based not on the reasoning mind but on the senses, set out to give plastic expression to the blind, instinctive forces and uncontrollable pulsions that lie beneath the surface of consciousness. Since this is the prevailing trend of art today, it is only natural that the younger generation of painters should be more susceptible than their elders to a purely sensorial art; only natural, therefore, that they should see Monet's last works in a new light.

WATER LILIES AT GIVERNY, 1905. DEEMS TAYLOR COLLECTION, NEW YORK.

WISTERIA, 1919-1925. PAUL ROSENBERG AND CO., NEW YORK.

To them the great *Water Lilies* recently withdrawn from the seclusion of the studio at Giverny have come as a revelation. In these canvases, executed when Monet's eyes were clouded by cataract, they have found, as it were, the sponsorship of their own experiments in "abstract expressionism." But the question arises: may not this apparent sponsorship be simply fortuitous, inasmuch as the works on which it is based were the result,

THE WATER-GARDEN AT GIVERNY. MUSÉE DES BEAUX-ARTS, GRENOBLE.

involuntary perhaps, of failing eyesight? To this there is only one reply: after the operation which partially restored his sight, Monet preserved the canvases in question instead of destroying them, and it was his lifelong habit to destroy every canvas that failed to satisfy him.

Furthermore, the keen interest he took in these experiments in near-abstraction, in which the very shape of objects melts away in modulations of colors, is confirmed by his deliberate resumption of them after his recovery. It is easy to identify the canvases executed before his operation, when the cataract had spread an amber-colored film over the crystalline lens of his eyes: these canvases are not only woolly in outline but abnormally yellow in tone. Those painted after the operation, on the contrary, have an almost acid freshness of tone. Now some of the latter group, some of the most characteristic among them in fact (whose documented dating, moreover, is unimpugnable), nevertheless retain a haziness of outline which renders the subjects unrecognizable. These works can only be regarded as experiments in abstraction deliberately undertaken.

Among these irrefutable examples of deliberate abstraction is a *Garden in Bloom*, in green and acid pink, whose subject is only recognizable by reference to a second version, painted by Monet at the same time, from the same spot, but with normal eyesight. The composition, angle of vision, lighting and color scheme of the two pictures are identical. The only difference is the handling, the focus, if you will: clean-cut in one, blurred in the other. Without reference to the first, which corresponds to it in every particular, save handling, the second fails to convey any figurative impression at all; it is, purely and simply, a magnificent symphony of colors.

If, for Monet, the line between the figurative and the abstract was so thin that it was a simple matter of handling for him to pass from one to the other, this means that even when figurative his canvases are an organization of colors quite as much as a representation of objects. Such is the distinctive feature of the last *Water Lilies*, which, while unquestionably representational paintings, yet attain a musicality of form and color sufficient

THE WATER-GARDEN AT GIVERNY. MICHEL MONET COLLECTION, SOREL-MOUSSEL.

to justify them independently of the subject. This fusion of realism and lyricism was the great achievement of Monet's old age, and the fulfillment of his Impressionism.

It was, moreover, a much more logical fulfillment than is generally realized. To assume that the Impressionists expressly chose to limit painting to the representation of reality is to misconstrue the impressionist esthetic. The problem they tackled lay elsewhere—it lay within themselves. Not only did they entertain no preconceived ideas on the subject of "reality," but their only interest in it was the sense impressions it supplied them with.

This attitude was dictated by a conviction that art is nothing without sincerity, without integrity. Realizing how prone we are, all of us, to smother spontaneous perception and sensation under an overgrowth of habits and preconceptions, they made a point of trusting entirely to their direct sensorial experience of objects. To this desire to drink at the source was added the determination to purify their vision of everything alien to it. It is common knowledge that, in our usual manner of looking at the world, we rely heavily on memory and *recognize* objects rather than *see* them. The Impressionists put out of mind what they knew by experience of the object before them and painted, as accurately as they could, only the features and colors it presented to their eye.

Several times, in plain words, Monet voiced this will to ignore the identity of what he painted and to render the colors he saw in front of him. And this is exactly what he did in actual practice: he colored in the entire canvas almost at once, then worked it up by the progressive modulation of the whole, without defining particular elements. The shimmering color texture of the last *Water Lilies* is indeed the logical outcome of this purely sensorial realism which seizes on the visual sensation and detaches it from all mental preconceptions.

VICISSITUDES OF CLAUDE MONET

*N*ow *that the second half of the 20th century is nearly a decade old, those of us who respond to the most radical experiments of present-day painting cannot help shrinking a little when it comes to reassessing an art so clearly labeled as Monet's is. A host of memories crowd in upon the mind—the commercial success of his work at the end of his life unaccompanied by any real understanding of it, the systematic disparagement of Monet by the Cubists, the exploitation of his achievement, after his death, for academic purposes—and interfere with the objective effort to fit Monet into his rightful place in the historical pattern. They are liable to interfere even more with the subjective appreciations of the disinterested lover of painting, who enjoys pictures without troubling himself about the historical context.*

*To put it bluntly, Monet almost inevitably appears to us now as the most eminent, most accomplished representative of an art movement that has had its day and gone out of fashion. As we all know, his was a major contribution to a long, patiently elaborated evolution of artistic taste and style at the end of which we stand today, confident that a kind of progress has been made (though the notion of progress seems to us wholly inapplicable to the plastic arts), and without which we simply would not be the kind of people we are. The fact remains, nevertheless, that Monet and his achievement are part and parcel of the 1900 esthetic (*art nouveau, Jugendstil, *"modern style," call it what you will) and of everything that, from 1870 on, paved the way for it.*

But it is also true that the 1900 esthetic is gradually being rehabilitated, resurrected from the grave to which we thought it had been consigned forever. We are coming to regard that period with a little less condescension and a little more respect. The day is not far off when we shall actually do it justice. Perhaps we feel sufficiently detached from it now to consider and evaluate it with something like objectivity—in other words, we no longer smile or blush at the 1900 esthetic, but rank it now, in the perspective of fifty years, among the arts and artists deserving of serious study in the museums. In time we may venture to admire it openly.

Now this trend of taste is all in Monet's favor, predisposing us as it does to a better understanding of his later work.

Cubism, by general consent, was a movement whose significance can hardly be overestimated. As things stand today, however, certain reservations have to be made. We all recognize the genius of its leaders and appreciate its masterpieces; we feel the sincerest esteem, indeed the most affectionate admiration for it. But Cubism henceforth belongs to history. It intervenes less and less in the issues at stake today; and even where it does intervene, it is no longer a greater force to be reckoned with than Impressionism is. In the family tree of ancestors of modern art—bearing in mind not the quality of the works themselves, but only the stimulative power of their influence—Impressionism, anyhow Monet's Impressionism, is about to oust Cubism from the privileged position it has occupied up to now. Hence Monet's irresistible return to favor at the present time. His stock is on the rise, and it may be predicted that it will continue to rise, for in his last works Monet came to grips with one of the thorniest problems of present-day art.

His greatness will be more generally realized when it is finally seen that Cézanne, for all the depth of his pictorial analyses, was not the only father of modern art; that Gauguin too had his share in that vast parentage; and that Claude Monet (less obviously but no less effectively) was instrumental in deflecting painting from the beaten path and projecting it toward new destinies.

The adepts of what is known as "lyrical abstraction" (though it is no more lyrical than any other kind and might more properly be designated "informal" or "anti-geometric" abstraction) are inclined to dismiss the so-called geometric abstractionists as belated followers of Mondrian, whose experiments in Neo-Plasticism (he himself called it Neue Gestaltung*) date as far back as 1917.*

The geometrics, on the other hand, might logically accuse the lyrical abstractionists of merely being the offspring of Kandinsky in his Fauve period of about 1910.

In neither case, to my mind, does the parentage in any way invalidate the achievement of the offspring. The latter are necessarily the offspring of someone, but not necessarily duplicates or facsimiles of their parents. The point I wish to make, however, is this: the immediate parentage in both cases masks an ancestor whom everyone finds it convenient to overlook, and that ancestor is Claude Monet.

One man has had the honesty to acknowledge it, a man of exceptional lucidity and foresight: Kandinsky himself. His statement of the facts is to be found in Rückblick, *an autobiographical essay first published by* Der Sturm *in 1913. It is essential to quote the passage in its entirety. At the turn of the century (the exact year is not mentioned) Kandinsky saw a* Haystack *by Monet at an exhibition of impressionist paintings.*

"My experience until then had been limited to naturalistic art, and almost exclusively to that of the Russians. I had sometimes remained a long while looking at the hand of Franz Liszt in Repin's portrait, among others, and now I suddenly found myself for the first time in front of a painting which, according to the catalogue, represented a haystack, but which I failed to recognize as such. This unintelligibility perplexed and worried me a good deal. I felt that the artist had no right to paint in so vague a way. I dimly realized that the object (the subject) was lacking in this picture. But I found with amazement and misgivings that the picture not only took one by surprise, but that it impressed itself indelibly on the memory and took shape again in the mind's eye

down to the last detail. All this I realized obscurely and could not yet foresee the natural consequences of this discovery. But one thing was brought home to me, and that was the unbelievable power, unlike anything I had ever known, of a palette that surpassed my wildest dreams. Painting struck me as being endowed with a fabulous power. But unconsciously I ceased to attach any importance, as an indispensable element, to the 'object' employed in the picture."

Such was the reaction of Kandinsky to one of Monet's later canvases, and at a time when Kandinsky was by no means predisposed in favor of modern art, but was as yet familiar with nothing bolder than the *19th-century Russian art of men like Repin.*

Now it would be unfair to suppose that Kandinsky, as he looked at this Haystack, was simply the dupe of his own imagination. Everything we know about him testifies to his perfect level-headedness, to the unfailing objectivity of his mental processes. And if Kandinsky no doubt read something of his future self into Monet's picture, at the same time he discerned much of what Monet himself projected into it. For both men were tending toward the same problem, both yearned for an art which can only be described as a sublimation of painting, and Monet's trend in this direction, even before the Water Lilies, was sufficiently marked for Kandinsky, with his keen insight, to discern it and be struck by it.

Today the wheel has turned full circle. The dreams and imaginings that haunted Kandinsky some sixty years ago have largely materialized. A whole domain of art that was mysterious and problematic then has now been pioneered and opened up. But to experience something of what he felt when he first saw that Haystack by Monet, we have only to recall our own initiation into abstract art, our own feelings of wonder and amazement years ago before this or that impressionist canvas.

To experience all these sensations we need go no farther than the work of Monet himself, for example the great Water Lilies of *1918-1919*. Monet at that time may still have shared the general belief that he was "only an eye," only a recording mechanism extraordinarily sensitive to *the most evanescent nuances of light and color. The canvases he was painting, however, suggest that he had gone beyond that stage. They suggest a mystery in his career, and the possibility arises that, to justify his boldness, he continued to describe as "visual impressions" what he knew to be the pure creations of his own mind. At a time when the observation of nature was still the golden rule of pictorial decorum, would he have ventured to describe his work as pure creation? The time was not yet ripe, and Monet must have realized that any such claim would have stigmatized him as a lunatic in the eyes of the world.*

There is a Monet mystery, and it seems probable that at the time Kandinsky was the only one to suspect it.

But Monet's secret has not escaped the notice of some of the younger men who came after Kandinsky. By devious means, perhaps, they too have been led to suspect its existence. The rankling, unavowed, enigmatic aspirations of Monet's old age are being rediscovered, re-experienced today by the younger generation of painters. But whereas Monet forged into the unknown with an abiding sense of risk and insecurity, present-day painters are ranging over it and eagerly recording the results of their explorations. Monet opened up the path which the newcomers are now reconnoitering, step by step.

Academic criticism would condemn certain canvases by Monet as wrong-headed, extravagant, insane, were it not for the fact that they bear his reassuring signature. And how many of the younger critics and writers, on the contrary, would be singing the praises of these same canvases, if only they were signed by some present-day abstractionist (none of whom can vie with Monet), while as it is they dismiss them out of hand as the work of a "mere Impressionist."

The fashion today, in the studios of some of the younger painters, is all for "textural" composition. They forget that even before they were born Monet set a standard of dense, shimmering, luxuriant surface textures that has yet to be surpassed. All based, it is true, on a vision of "nature." But what about the inspiration of the abstractionists and tachistes? *May it not be ultimately traceable to the same source?*

Just how much, moreover, do we really know about the ultimate source of Monet's inspiration? What did he think of the new schools of painting on the rise at the end of his life? Was he really, at Giverny, so completely out of touch with contemporary painting as we are led to believe?

One thing is certain: Monet stands out today as the involuntary prophet of the younger generation, just as Cézanne stood out as the involuntary prophet of the cubist generation. This is a fact and it is only fair to acknowledge it.

LÉON DEGAND.

SELECTED BIBLIOGRAPHY

EXHIBITIONS

INDEX OF NAMES

LIST OF COLORPLATES

CONTENTS

SELECTED BIBLIOGRAPHY

No catalogue of Monet's paintings has yet been published; a catalogue is being prepared by Daniel Wildenstein. — An exhaustive study of Monet is being prepared by Professor William C. Seitz of Princeton University.

Correspondence

No complete edition of the correspondence exists. Letters to Paul Durand-Ruel (411) and Octave Maus (6) were published by L. VENTURI in *Les Archives de l'Impressionnisme*, Paris-New York 1939; to Boudin in G. CAHEN, *E. Boudin, sa vie et son œuvre*, Paris 1900; to Bazille in G. POULAIN, *Bazille et ses amis*, Paris 1932, and F. DAULTE, *Frédéric Bazille et son temps*, Geneva 1952; to Duret in T. DURET, *Histoire d'Edouard Manet et de son œuvre*, Paris 1902; to Manet in A. TABARANT, *Autour de Manet*, in *L'Art Vivant*, May 4, 1928; to Chocquet in J. JOËTS, *Les Impressionnistes et Chocquet*, in *L'Amour de l'Art*, April 1935; to Berthe Morisot in D. ROUART, *Correspondance de Berthe Morisot*, Paris 1950; to Emile Zola, quoted in J. REWALD, *Cézanne, sa vie, son œuvre, son amitié pour Zola*, Paris 1939.

Witness Accounts and Reminiscences

E. TABOUREAUX, *Claude Monet*, in *La Vie Moderne*, June 12, 1880. — T. ROBINSON, *Claude Monet*, in *Century Magazine*, September 1892. — M. GUILLEMET, *Claude Monet*, in *Revue Illustrée*, March 15, 1898. — THIÉBAULT-SISSON, *Claude Monet, un entretien*, in *Le Temps*, November 27, 1900 (an important interview). — L. VAUXCELLES, *Un Après-midi chez Claude Monet*, in *L'Art et les Artistes*, December 1905. — W. PACH, *Interview with Monet*, in *Scribner's Magazine*, 1908. — M. ELDER, *Chez Claude Monet à Giverny*, Paris 1924. — Duc de TRÉVISE, *Le pèlerinage de Giverny*, in *Revue de l'Art Ancien et Moderne*, January-February 1927. — R. GIMPEL, *At Giverny with Claude Monet*, in *Art in America*, June 1927. — L. C. PERRY, *Reminiscences of Claude Monet from 1889 to 1909*, in *The American Magazine of Art*, March 1927.

Monographs and Albums

O. MIRBEAU, *Claude Monet, "Venise"*, Paris 1912. — A. ALEXANDRE, *Claude Monet*, Paris 1921. — G. GEFFROY, *Claude Monet, sa vie, son temps, son œuvre*, Paris 1922 (an important study, well documented but confused). — C. MAUCLAIR, *Claude Monet*, Paris 1924. — F. FELS, *Claude Monet*, Paris 1925 and 1927. — F. FOSCA, *Claude Monet*, Paris 1927. — L. GILLET, *Trois Études sur Claude Monet*, Paris 1928. — G. CLEMENCEAU, *Claude Monet, Les Nymphéas*, Paris 1928. — L. WERTH, *Claude Monet*, Paris 1928. — M. DE FELS, *La vie de Claude Monet*, Paris 1929. — Lady LATHOM, *Claude Monet*, London 1931-New York 1932. — S. GWYNN, *Claude Monet and his Garden*, London 1934. — G. GRAPPE, *Monet*, Paris 1941. — M. MALINGUE,

Claude Monet, Monaco 1941 and 1943. — H. ROSTRUP, *Claude Monet et ses tableaux dans les collections danoises*, Copenhagen 1941. — A. M. CETTO, *Claude Monet*, Basel 1943 and 1947. — O. REUTERSWAERD, *Monet*, Stockholm 1948. — C. SCHWEICHER, *Monet*, Bern 1949. — C. ROGER-MARX, *Monet*, Lausanne 1949. — C. LÉGER, *Claude Monet*, Paris 1950. — G. BESSON, *Claude Monet*, Paris 1951. — P. WESTHEIM, *Claude Monet*, Zurich 1953.

Chief Magazine Articles

A. DE LOSTALOT, *Exposition des œuvres de M. Claude Monet*, in *Gazette des Beaux-Arts* I, 1883. — O. MIRBEAU, *Claude Monet*, in *L'Art dans les Deux Mondes*, March 7, 1891. — A. FONTAINAS, *Claude Monet*, in *Mercure de France*, May 1899. — A. ALEXANDRE, *Claude Monet, His Career and Work*, in *The Studio*, March 1908. — R. KOECHLIN, *Claude Monet*, in *Art et Décoration*, February 1927. — R. REGAMEY, *La Formation de Claude Monet*, in *Gazette des Beaux-Arts*, February 1927. — P. JAMOT, *A propos de l'exposition Monet*, in *Bulletin des Musées*, 1931, pp. 118-123. — G. POULAIN, *L'Origine des Femmes au jardin de Claude Monet*, in *L'Amour de l'Art*, March 1937. — F. ARCANGELI, *Monet*, in *Paragone*, No. 31, 1952, pp. 54-61. — G. BACHELARD, *Les Nymphéas ou Les surprises d'une nuit d'été*, in *Verve* VII, 27-28, 1952, p. 59. — A. MASSON, *Monet le fondateur*, in *Verve* VII, 27-28, 1952, p. 68. — K. H. USENER, *Claude Monets Seerosen-Wandbilder in der Orangerie*, in *Wallraf-Richartz Jahrbuch*, Cologne 1952, XIV, p. 216-225. — W. C. SEITZ, *Monet and Abstract Painting*, in *College Art Journal*, 1956, 1, p. 34-46. — C. GREENBERG, *Later Monet*, in *Art News Annual*, 1957, p. 132-148.

EXHIBITIONS

Salons of 1865 (two seascapes), 1866 (one portrait, one landscape), 1868 (one seascape), 1880 (one landscape). — Group Exhibitions of the Impressionists: 1874 (5 items), 1876 (18 items), 1877 (31 items), 1879 (29 items), 1882 (25 items).

1880, June, in the offices of the review "La Vie Moderne," 7, Boulevard des Italiens, Paris (18 items, preface by Théodore Duret). — 1883, March 1-25, Galerie Durand-Ruel, Paris (56 items). — 1884, April, Galerie Georges Petit, Paris. — 1885, Galerie Georges Petit, Paris. — 1886, spring, Société des Vingt, Brussels. — 1886, May-July, Galerie Georges Petit, Paris. — 1888, July, Galerie Boussod et Valadon, Paris (10 Antibes seascapes). — 1889, Goupil Gallery, London (20 items). — 1889, June, Monet-Rodin Exhibition, Galerie Georges Petit, Paris (66 items, preface by Octave Mirbeau). — 1891, May, Galerie Durand-Ruel, Paris (22 items, including 15 *Haystacks*). — 1892, February 29-March 10, Galerie Durand-Ruel, Paris (15 items, including 6 *Poplars*). — 1895, May 10-31, Galerie Durand-Ruel, Paris (50 items, including 20 *Cathedrals*). — 1897, February, Stockholm. — 1897, summer, Second International Biennale, Venice (20 items). — 1898, June, Galerie Georges Petit, Paris (61 items, including 24 *Cliffs* and 18 *Mornings on the Seine*). — 1900, November 22-December 15, Galerie Durand-Ruel, Paris (first series of *Water Lilies*). — 1902, February, 21-28, Galerie Bernheim-Jeune, Paris (6 *Views of Vétheuil*). — 1904, May 9-June 4, Galerie Durand-Ruel, Paris (37 *Views of the Thames*). — 1909, May 6-June 5, Galerie Durand-Ruel, Paris (48 *Water Lilies*). — 1912, May 25-June 8, Galerie Bernheim-Jeune, Paris (29 *Views of Venice*). — 1921, January 21-February 2, Galerie Durand-Ruel, Paris. — 1928, February, Galerie Thannhauser, Berlin. — 1931, Musée de l'Orangerie, Paris. — 1940, Centenary Monet-Rodin, Musée de l'Orangerie, Paris. — 1945, April-May, Galerie Wildenstein, New York. — 1952, May 10-June 15, Kunsthaus, Zurich (126 items, preface by George Besson). — 1952, June 19-July 17, Gazette des Beaux-Arts, Paris (75 items, preface by Daniel Wildenstein). — 1952, July 24-September 22, Municipal Museum, The Hague (90 items, preface by George Besson). — 1954, June-July, Marlborough Fine Art Gallery, London. — 1956, June, Galerie Katia Granoff, Paris *(Water Lilies)*. — 1956, October, Knoedler Gallery, New York. — 1957, May, Galerie Katia Granoff, Paris *(L'étang enchanté de Claude Monet)*. — 1957, The Royal Scottish Academy, Edinburgh, and The Tate Gallery, London (115 items, preface by Douglas Cooper). — 1957, City Art Museum, St Louis, and The Minneapolis Institute of Arts (103 items, preface by William C. Seitz).

INDEX OF NAMES

LIST OF COLORPLATES

On the Title Page:

The Floating Studio (fragment), c. 1874. Rijksmuseum Kröller-Müller, Otterlo.

On the Dustjacket:

The Beach at Trouville (detail), 1870. By Courtesy of the Tate Gallery, London.

The Water-Garden at Giverny (detail). Musée des Beaux-Arts, Grenoble.

CONTENTS

THIS VOLUME, THE TWENTY-FIFTH OF THE COLLECTION "THE
TASTE OF OUR TIME", WAS PRODUCED BY THE TECHNICAL STAFF
OF EDITIONS D'ART ALBERT SKIRA, FINISHED THE FIFTEENTH
DAY OF NOVEMBER, NINETEEN HUNDRED AND FIFTY-EIGHT.

TEXT AND ILLUSTRATIONS BY THE

COLOR STUDIO
AT IMPRIMERIES RÉUNIES S.A., LAUSANNE

PLATES ENGRAVED BY GUEZELLE ET RENOUARD, PARIS.

PHOTOGRAPHY

*Henry B. Beville, Washington (pages 37, 39, 42, 43, 53, 65, 68, 69, 72, 73, 74,
80, 82, 83, 85, 89, 91, 94, 97, 100, 103, 104), Louis Laniepce, Paris (pages 41,
59, 60, 63, 64, 79, 84, 107), Walter Steinkopf, Berlin (page 62), Zoltán Wegner,
London (page 92), Paul I. Bessem, Amsterdam (page 3). Other photographs were
obligingly lent by the Ny Carlsberg Glyptotek, Copenhagen (page 31) and by the magazine Du, Zurich (pages 28, 45, 56, 86, 90, 95, 105 and the reverse of the dustjacket).*

PRINTED IN SWITZERLAND